FI

by William Wister Haines

SLIM

HIGH TENSION

COMMAND DECISION

COMMAND DECISION

COMMAND DECISION

by *William Wister Haines*

AN ATLANTIC MONTHLY PRESS BOOK

LITTLE, BROWN AND COMPANY · BOSTON

1947

Published January 1947
Reprinted January 1947

To

JOHN WISTER HAINES

and

GRANT BARNEY SCHLEY

who died in the service of their country

Author's Note

This story is a novel; by definition, "fictitious prose narrative of sufficient length to fill one or more volumes portraying characters and actions representative of real life in continuous plot."

Use of the name of any person living or dead, excepting named public figures, is unintentional coincidence.

W. W. H.

COMMAND DECISION

Chapter One

ELMER BROCKHURST drove up to the gate of the Fifth Division Headquarters with deeper emotion than he would have disclosed to any of his fellow war correspondents in London. Pride had been stirring in him all the way up the Great North Road that led from the metropolis like the trunk of a tree to the branching, budding American air bases in the flat middle counties. To enter an American station was to come home. The glow inside him was intensified rather than diminished by the knowledge that he personally would be unwelcome here.

Brockhurst had quarreled with officialdom through five campaigns. A powerful syndicate kept him because he won a satisfactory proportion of the quarrels. Today he knew he would be fighting his own people in a good old-fashioned family row.

The expression of the young corporal on guard confirmed this pleasant presentiment even before the boy spoke.

"You're forbidden the station, Mr. Brockhurst. Orders."

Then, to modify the severity of this pronouncement, the boy smiled confidentially.

"The Old Man's got his tail over the dashboard."

Brockhurst produced his new pass and watched the young face pucker with perplexity.

3

"Just a minute, sir. The sergeant he gets paid more than I do for handling hot ones."

He went into the guard box. Brockhurst waited, studying the station with a practiced eye. This particular Division H. Q. had its little nucleus of buildings across the perimeter track from an operational group — the standard, ugly brick rectangles carved with the crazy angles of camouflage, and beyond them the loaf-shaped roofs of the Nissens nestling along the hedgerows. A dispirited volleyball game was in progress on the sandy flat.

His mind was on business as his eyes followed the long oval of the perimeter track, a two-mile enclosure of emerald grass slashed and crisscrossed with runways. At the first sight of it Brockhurst nodded to himself. The black, oil-stained parking stands that studded its outer rim like teeth on a gear wheel were barren. The great greenish beetles that waddled and snorted here through darkness and half-light had vanished for the day.

The somnolent drone of a few motors from the gaping hangars told of the unhurried testing. A mile above him a ragged barb of six planes orbited slowly through what was evidently a much needed formation practice. And miles above them, he suspected, was another single plane circling with monotonous steadiness through the subzero altitudes to freeze the Group's ice cream for supper.

Brockhurst saw that the ambulance and crash trucks were drawn up in meticulous formation by the Operations tower. But their motors were idle, the asbestos suits were still laid out on fenders, the crews not yet assembled. There was a mission out all right, a big one. But under the soft rare sunlight of a brilliant summer day the station drowsed.

4

Studying it more slowly now, Brockhurst wondered
what it was that made this pastoral patch of Lincolnshire
America. It was more than the drooping flag over Division Headquarters, more than the velocity of the occasional jeeps, more than the accent or attitude of the guard.
With the English it was teatime; for no more trouble than
driving to the cook shack he could shortly be drinking all
the good coffee he wanted.

What he was feeling was not as simple as the smell of
coffee, however. He was remembering an old saying:
you could take the boy out of the country but you
couldn't take the country out of the boy. That was what
made this place, all these places, America. Brockhurst had
seen this happen in both hemispheres, on both sides of the
equator. The army simply took the country along with
it.

His reverie was interrupted by the sergeant.

"I guess it's okay, Mr. Brockhurst. That's General
Kane's signature all right."

He returned the pass with a final, awed glance. Then,
duty done, he, like the corporal, lowered his voice for a
pleased confidence.

"When Dennis sees you he'll spit a snake."

2

At four that afternoon Technical Sergeant
Harold Evans had relieved his assistant, Corporal Herbert McGinnis, in the office of General Dennis with a
sense of buoyant well-being. He had just had almost five
hours of uninterrupted sack. He had had four fresh eggs
and an orange in the combat mess. He had a date with

Joan at the White Hart at seven and he thought the chances of keeping it were good. After missions like yesterday's and today's the General wouldn't send them tomorrow. With the board scrubbed Evans was a cinch for at least six hours off.

He wanted six hours for his deal. Eddie Cahill, who was line chief at the 641st Group, had offered Evans three pounds ten to give Joan the gate. Like most of the men that worked on the line Eddie was always behind the eight ball with girls. In the first place he never had much time. When he got a break from the weather he still couldn't get his hands clean, even by scrubbing the skin off with high octane.

Joan was not fastidious but the night Evans and Eddie had met her she had whispered to Evans that she didn't like a man who smelt like a bloody petrol tin. But now Evans was tired of her and Eddie knew it.

She was a good girl as they went but six weeks were six weeks. When Evans showed signs of being fed up Eddie made the timely suggestion that a transfer of her affections to himself would be worth three pounds ten.

Evans didn't care much about the money but then neither did Eddie, especially since half the guys on the 641st line worked for their chief's dice. What Evans did want was some whiskey. He'd have to be looking around again and whiskey always made an impression on these girls. Evans knew a flight engineer in the Air Transport Command who was going to Belfast next week. Three pounds ten was a reaming for John Jameson but this way it would be a free bottle.

Evans was still annoyed with the General's drinking

6

habits. At the moment it happened to be his only grievance and he cherished it accordingly.

When he had finished his missions Evans had thought himself lucky at the chance to become the General's sergeant. He had been compelled to choose, fast, between that and Personnel. Headquarters certainly meant indoor work and better food and transportation than he was likely to get elsewhere. And traditionally it should have meant plenty of liquor. Evans had accepted only to discover that General Dennis rarely drank. The single bottle of whiskey in his desk was reserved for the visits of Colonel Martin, and they both knew how much Colonel Martin drank and when.

Otherwise the job was all right. General Dennis was real army, even to that ring; curt, crisp, predictable. He was distant and took his job hard. But on the whole Evans had nothing against the General except the deplorable drought in the office, a drought that was partly compensated by Mrs. Dennis's regular shipments of the best cigars Evans had ever tasted.

As soon as he had taken over the office Evans put on the General's coffee and then studied his watch. The General had not gone to the sack until eleven. The boys would scarcely be back for another hour. It seemed a fairly safe bet that he'd be alone for thirty minutes. He went over to the desk and selected one of Dennis's cigars with loving care. As a precaution before lighting it he hung the CONFERENCE DO NOT DISTURB sign on the anteroom door.

Evans seated himself within reach of the coffeepot on the stove and lit the cigar with expanding content. He

7

knew the boys were having it rough today but he couldn't help it and no one had cried for him while he was doing his twenty-five. By now they should be almost back to the fighters anyway and from there in was a good bet, even on three motors.

There hadn't been any fighter cover through most of Evans's twenty-five missions and for a time after the end of his tour he had enjoyed pointing out to the replacement crews that the war was getting soft. Lately he did not mention this so often. The new crews had an uncomfortable way of reminding him that he'd done most of his over France. Dennis seemed to have forgotten there was a France.

Evans filled his big lungs with the delectable fragrance of the cigar and lifted his feet comfortably up onto the General's map table. Then he dropped them softly and tensed as he saw the anteroom door swinging silently open. Anyone who barged through that sign should be big. His apprehension changed to outraged indignation as he perceived that it was only Elmer Brockhurst.

3

Brockhurst had barged in so boldly because he had learned over his coffee in the cook shack that the General was still asleep. Audacity had done a lot for Brockhurst in life; he had hoped it would be good for a look at the map board in the General's office this afternoon.

Finding Evans on duty only sharpened his hungry scrutiny of the room. The maps and operational status boards were properly masked behind their heavy draw curtains. Brockhurst had been afraid of this; he well knew the working, as distinguished from the official, rule that the lower the echelon the higher the security. Lieutenant generals regularly told and showed him things lieutenants would have been busted for mentioning.

Divisions were relatively small units in the expanding Air Forces. The brigadier generals who commanded them were usually obscure, mostly conscientious, and often capable. The office of this particular one was the usual barren rectangle of damp brick.

Through the Ops room door across the office Brockhurst could hear the muffled clattering of the teleprinter. The rack of Tommy guns, the General's tin hat, gas mask, and service automatic hanging neatly behind the big bare desk, reflected not only the apprehension inherent in all Army Regulations but the wistful hope of all headquarters staffs that something might conceivably happen. The phones on the desk — black for Admin, green for Secrecy, red for Ops — were proof that to and from this dreary room there would be a great deal of talk.

The big windows with blackout curtains now neatly cuffed back commanded the perimeter track, runways, and, across the oval, the squat buildings of the operational group that used this station. The wall ornaments were as standard as GI soap. That Fortress propeller had unquestionably been removed from the first plane in the Division to survive twenty-five missions. The unmounted Browning .50 was as certainly the first in the Division to have shot down a German plane. The converted peanut tins on desk and map table were well into a second tour of duty as ash trays.

In a corner a carefully arranged cluster of British, American, and Division flags drooped over a squat, sturdy chest clearly stenciled "Division Flag Locker." Brockhurst wondered whether the juxtaposition of flags, guns, and fire extinguishers represented some sergeant's conscious sense of irony or perhaps was so ordered in regulations.

Then he saw something new. From a previously blank patch of brick wall now blazed the black and white Swastika-shaped marking cross of a German fighter plane. It was authentic. Brockhurst had seen captured ones before. But he knew that Heavy Bombardment Divisions did not capture German planes. He had known it when, two days before, his startled eyes had seen this same marking cross on its own plane in Hangar Four just before the guard arrested him for snooping. For the moment he covered his excitement and forced his attention onto Evans, whose steady scrutiny had begun to make itself felt through the silence.

"Is the Old Man in, Sergeant?"

"Does it look like it?"

Brockhurst knew he'd asked for that one. The Sergeant's cigar dispelled any pretense that the General was around. But his manifest annoyance seemed to have thawed a little with the success of his crack, and that was something.

"Seriously, Joe, where's the Old Man?"

"My name isn't Joe. What old man?"

Brockhurst hesitated. Sometimes a note of contempt for the brass went a long way with these kids. Sometimes under their studied toughness were unfathomable depths of loyalty, even hero worship. This Evans was a mature,

10

self-reliant young man if Brockhurst had ever seen one. He smiled sardonically.

"Brigadier General K. C. Dennis, Commanding General of the Fifth American Bombardment Division, Heavy. Don't all good sergeants call their generals 'the Old Man'?"

Leaving Evans to chew that one over, Brockhurst walked calmly over to the fighter-plane marking cross. Assurance went a long way with the army. He had just begun a closer study of the cross when he heard Evans's even voice.

"Who let you in here?"

He continued his silent, absorbed examination.

"Who let you in here?"

"I can't hear you, Sergeant," he said over his shoulder.

Then he did hear the hard ominous steps, the hands on the Tommy gun, the clatter of a hand-ejected shell on the bare floor. He turned to find himself looking into the muzzle of the gun. The safety was forward.

The trigger pull on those guns was notoriously light, as light as the balance of impulses in that poker-faced boy who was pointing it squarely at his stomach. Too late he realized that he had been wasting subtlety on a barbarian. Brockhurst wet his lips.

"Look out. That thing might go off."

"*Might* hell. Who let you in here?"

"I've got a pass."

"I seen Dennis tear it up. A man without no pass is a spy."

Evans had intended only to scare some of the condescension out of Brockhurst. It was the correspondent's own manifest fear which now showed him the possibili-

11

ties of the situation. He could teach the whole nosy breed of them a lesson with no risk whatever to himself. A man without a pass was a spy. He noted the sweat on Brockhurst's forehead and thought aloud.

"Perry Machold over in the 291st MP's he got the Soldier's Medal for shooting at a guy that they didn't even know if he was a spy and Perry missed him. I bet Dennis'd give me a Bronze Star."

Brockhurst gulped.

"I've got a new pass, from Dennis's boss."

"Walk your pass over here, slow."

Brockhurst extended it with exaggerated slowness over the Tommy-gun muzzle and listened while Evans muttered through a careful reading of the simple sentence.

". . . signed . . . who?"

"Major General R. G. Kane, that's who."

Evans nodded, awed in spite of himself. "Imagine that? A goddamned old Major General probably gets as much money as a fair-to-middling third baseman and can't sign his own name clear enough to read. Yeah, that's old Percent himself."

"Why do you boys call him that?" Brockhurst knew very well but there was safety in continuing the distraction.

"Because of that crap he puts in the papers about the percentage of Germany his gallant forces destroy every afternoon, weather permitting."

Evans returned the pass, racked the Tommy gun, resumed his seat, and puffed hard to restore the fading ember of his cigar. Brockhurst resisted a wish to wipe his forehead with his handkerchief and sat down beside the Sergeant, keeping his eyes ostentatiously from that fighter-plane marking.

"You know the score," said Brockhurst. "When I get through with that low-grade Fascist megalomaniac . . ."

"With who?"

"Dennis. That's what he is, a low-grade Fascist mega-lomaniac."

"What's that?"

Brockhurst considered judicially. "He's an ex-test pilot who's been brought indoors to a job way over his head and still thinks if he makes enough records with other people's lives and blood no one will find out what a hollow-headed humbug he is."

"How long you been around the army?"

"Long enough to know that's what Dennis is."

"That's what all generals are," said Evans. "Coffee?"

Brockhurst welcomed this first intimation of cordial-ity. This sergeant probably knew every detail of the story he wanted.

"Where is Dennis, Sarge?"

"In the sack."

"I see. After a sleepless night of planning, the gallant commander snatches a few winks while his men are out on the mission."

"You must love that guardhouse, pumping me about missions."

Brockhurst snorted. "Security! Even the hangar queens patched up and gone today but I'm not supposed to know there's a mission out."

"If you know, what are you hinting for?"

"Angles," said Brockhurst. "I know the hottest story in the war when I smell it but two or three angles to fill

13

in the picture would be worth plenty to me." Brock-hurst lowered his voice persuasively.

"I know he's got the German plane that Swastika came from under close guard in Hangar Four. And I know he's flown it himself, several times."

"You know more than that," Evans encouraged him.

"You're damned right I do."

"You know he throwed your ass in the guardhouse for writing a piece about it and kept the piece and tore up your pass."

The sergeant burst into a triumphant chuckle. Brock-hurst waited patiently for it to subside.

"I got out," he said. "And I've got a new pass from General Kane. That guardhouse was a break for me. But I still want to know what became of the German Dennis had in there."

"What are the other angles?"

"Why has Dennis been to London so often lately?"

Evans yawned. "Why does anyone go to London?"

"Not that Puritanical bastard," said Brockhurst. "Then yesterday, without even alerting us, Dennis runs off the longest mission of the war and has the worst losses to date. We try to help you guys take the curse off it with a good story and you won't even give us the target. 'Industrial Objectives!' That's a fine comfort to a lot of new widows back home."

"Go on."

"This morning everything that could roll to the end of the runway went earlier and they aren't back yet. Maximum effort, deep in Germany, two days straight. For what?"

"Why don't you ask some smart newspaperman?"

Frustration made Brockhurst's voice edgy. "Those jerks are still waiting permission to go to bases. They think this is just a routine mission."

"What makes you think it isn't?"

"Because I get paid for using my head instead of Public Relations handouts." He let this sink in and then barked, "Why has Dennis got a squadron commander with a D.F.C. under close arrest right now in the same guardhouse where they had me?"

"Not brushing his teeth?"

"Okay, my helpful friend, I'll tell you. He's there for refusing to go on this hush-hush mission this morning."

Evans's jaw muscles tightened now. "Did he tell you that?"

"Rafferty won't let me talk to him. And I suppose Dennis will back him up. But if that little tin-star tyrant thinks the American press will stand for this . . ."

"By God, you might be worth a Legion of Merit," said Evans and shifted his glance pointedly to the Tommy guns.

Brockhurst snorted. "You won't get it from Dennis. Cliff Garnett sat down at Prestwick last night by special plane."

"Who's he?"

"You never heard of Brigadier General Clifton C. Garnett, Secretary to the United Chiefs of Staff?"

"Oh God! Now we'll never get the war over," said Evans.

"I'll bet you Dennis's war is over in a week."

"You reckon they'd trade him for one of them Pentagon bellhops?"

"Garnett should have had this job to begin with."

15

Evans had heard of generals being fired but there was something about all this that didn't quite fit. Remembering, he shook his head firmly.

"They can't. They never fired no general yet till they give him the Legion of Merit, or if it was bad enough the D.S.M. Dennis, he hasn't got neither."

"They can give 'em mighty quick. Going to miss your hero?"

"He's no hero to me. I just taken this job in with the big wheels to chisel myself a ticket to China now I'm done with this war. Does this Garnett drink whiskey or Scotch?"

Brockhurst leaned forward gravely, confidentially.

"Listen, Sarge, Dennis is washed up. Trouble with the press, record losses yesterday and probably again today, a hero in the guardhouse; he's a ruptured duck, boy. But a couple of angles on this deal would be worth some good bourbon to me."

"What angles?"

"What became of that German Dennis had in the guardhouse?"

"Bonded bourbon?"

"Bottled in bond."

"How much?"

"Four bottles."

Evans's face darkened with indignation. "You give Rafferty in the guardhouse two cases, just for having his girl in the village make that phone call that got you out."

"I did like hell. I gave Peterson one case . . ." Brockhurst shut his mouth, too late. He had set too many verbal traps himself not to feel the click of this one. "Okay, call it a case — for the whole story, though."

16

Evans looked cautiously at both doors, removed the cigar from his mouth, and leaned forward. Brockhurst's ears stretched.

"Dennis kept him there till last night. But yesterday they was a SNAFU at the Quartermaster's and he run clean out of Spam. The General he said by God he'd promised the men meat for breakfast and if they wasn't no other meat we'd just have to use that Kraut. If you could have heard them boys at breakfast bitching about the meat packers' profiteering. . . ."

Brockhurst arose, livid. "Okay, you got your joke and I still got my whiskey."

Evans waited until the anteroom door banged shut on the correspondent. Then he jumped for the black phone on the General's desk. "Guardhouse. . . . Rafferty, give me Peterson. . . . Peterson, this is Evans. Bring six of them twelve marbles you just found to General Dennis's anteroom in a musette bag." He locked his lips over the cigar and revived the ember before cutting off the paean of protest that battered his eardrums. "You heard me . . . in twenty minutes. Well, Jesus Christ, I'm giving you half of 'em, ain't I?"

He hung up the phone and stretched his long arms with tingling satisfaction. His instinct had been right. Now, for a little patience, he not only had six immediate bottles of whiskey, he had discovered an operating procedure. It always took time to get onto a new job but he had the war under control again now.

Evans decided to give Joan outright to Eddie Cahill. Eddie had a tough time, as all dopes did, and Joan was good, if monotonous. He would give them a bottle of bourbon for a dowry, to end the thing without hard

17

feelings. The feeling of magnanimity, expanding with his new riches, was so pleasant that Evans extended it to Dennis. He was on easy street now, even if Dennis did get canned and this Garnett drank milk. War had many privations but there was no shortage of fools who wanted to talk to generals. He was thinking of them tenderly when the door opened and General Dennis walked in.

Chapter Two

GENERAL DENNIS returned to work that afternoon feeling a little better than usual. He had had nearly five hours of sleep — two troubled and fitful until they awoke him with the strike signal, then three of deep and blessed oblivion. His powdered-egg omelet had been no worse than usual and the arrival of a new consignment of canned grapefruit juice had brightened his meal after the Sergeant assured him there was enough for non-combat messes.

On the way over to the office he had noted that six of yesterday's crop of minor repairs were already restored to serviceability and practicing formation. It was a modest but tangible backlog against tomorrow.

But as his mind came fully to life again returning anxiety dispelled his momentary relief. It would be forty-odd minutes before he would know about his losses, either in the abstract or about Ted himself. In the meantime he had to get on with the Jenks case and whatever else had come up while he slept.

He noted the Sergeant's flustered jump to attention and noted also that the man had been smoking with his feet on the desk. That was normal; it was also normal for them to think they were fooling a man who didn't care. The click of the phone probably meant he had been phoning his girl in the village, but it might not.

"Was that for me?"

"No, sir," said Evans blandly.

Dennis was already crossing the room for a hurried look through the window at the sky he had not now studied for a full thirty seconds. He fired another question over his shoulder.

"Any word since the strike signal?"

"No, sir."

Dennis's eyes were lost in the sky. Gently Evans placed the partly smoked cigar in the ash tray on the desk. He made it safely, and then scrutinized the General at the window with a curiosity he had never felt about him until this afternoon. The idea that the General, like other mortals, could be fired reduced him to the kind of estimate used for human beings.

Evans saw a wiry, almost fragile figure, immaculately trim and erect with half a lifetime's habit of perfect posture. A lingering trace of shaving soap by the left ear almost matched the pallor of that bony face, with tight skin furrowed ten years deeper than its rightful forty. Not until this moment had Evans observed that Dennis always looked deeply, permanently tired. The sharpness of those deep-set gray eyes and the alertness of that trim figure camouflaged this fatigue most of the time. Seeing him in comparative repose now Evans was struck with the resemblance of his deep inner weariness to that he had noticed in older crew members toward the end of a tour. Without waiting to be asked he poured a cup of coffee and placed it on the desk.

Abruptly Dennis dismissed a sky he could not change and strode back to the desk. Evans held his breath. The General looked about him with a little frown of perplexity and then lifted the cigar to his mouth and in-

20

haled deeply. The General was all business now as he reached for the coffee.

"Ask Colonel Haley to step in, alert the weatherman, and have the guard bring Captain Jenks."

Evans vanished into the Ops room. Dennis reached into the top drawer of the desk and pulled out a Manila-covered file an inch thick. It was filled with orders, reports, certificates, judgments, records, qualifications; everything the Army of the United States considered worth remembering about Jenks, Lucius Malcolm, Capt. A. C., from its original satisfaction about the proportions of sugar and albumin in his urine right down to that ghastly moment this morning. Dennis had read the file through before sleeping. Now he only stared at it as if the cover might show him something the contents had not until Haley entered the room, saluting at the door.

The very sight of his Chief of Staff comforted Dennis but it was scarcely a personal emotion. Haley was solid gold and, like many forms of that substance, somewhat lumpy. He was painstaking about his uniforms but his appearance always suggested troublesome adenoids. Dennis leaned heavily on his tireless phlegmatic capability, but the relationship between them was more the product of custom than of written regulations.

These latter made Haley in fact Dennis's professional wife, who did multitudinous essential chores with skill and force, creating a serene efficient background which freed the commander's concentration for problems beyond the household. It was custom that could make this intimacy a brotherhood or a bondage. These two had served together only a relatively short time. Haley's own

21

notions of propriety and decorum kept the service rigid. Dennis had wondered at times if Haley, like himself, did not privately regret that the relationship was so inescapably functional. If so he never showed it. He never showed anything. He waited now, dutiful and attentive, for the moment when Dennis should be ready to give thought to the handful of papers he had brought. He always brought papers.

"Anything from the mission?"

"Just the strike signal I woke you for, as ordered, sir."

"Read it again."

Haley's pudgy fingers pulled the right paper nimbly out of the sheaf. He read without emotion.

" 'Primary plastered. Warm here. Martin.' "

" 'Warm' . . ." mused Dennis.

"Intelligence said they'd fight today, sir."

"But he says he plastered it, Haley."

"Yes, sir. And Colonel Martin is always conservative."

"Ted, conservative?" Dennis looked his astonishment.

Haley had said so because he thought so, but he knew what was the trouble. In the personal notebook in which he recorded his progress toward perfection there was an entry for Exactness and Accuracy of Speech against which he often had to give himself bad grades. Tonight he would have to mark up another one; meanwhile he amplified.

"On operational matters he is, sir. I've noticed it."

Dennis grunted. "I guess you're right. How's the board?"

Haley walked to the wall and pulled back one of the

22

curtain masks with relief. When the General was just talking it was impossible to tell where the conversation would lead or what might come up. The board was the purest, indisputable arithmetic.

Dennis followed him over now for a close scrutiny of the welter of crisscrossing chalk columns on the blackboard. He, too, knew it was purest arithmetic and accurate. Haley would have torn a strip off anyone guilty of a digit's error in it. Dennis, however, was thinking of the fallacy and futility of all arithmetic, of the hopelessness of trying to encompass what Bismarck had called the imponderables into arrangements of ten symbols.

Total war, however, was not his responsibility; the Fifth Division was. This board reflected, minute by minute, every demonstrable measurement of its operating condition. If Dennis had gone to it without question Haley would have stood behind him silently. Since he had asked about it, Haley read aloud the items of foremost concern.

"Thirteen Minor Repairs promised by fifteen hundred, eighteen promised from Major Repair by twenty-three hundred. Twenty-two Maidenheads from Modification arriving stations now. Thirty of those new ones weather-bound in Iceland took off at eleven hundred this morning. They're already modified and we should have them for tomorrow's board."

"That's final on yesterday's salvage?"

"Yes, sir. Ten to Major Repair, sixteen Category E."

"Sixteen . . ."

Haley could feel the sense of loss in Dennis's voice. He saw that the General was a little down, anyway, probably about that Jenks business. In the circumstances it seemed to him proper to point out the compensation.

"Of course Major Repair will cannibalize them for parts, sir. And there were only two killed in the crews."

Dennis nodded. "Are the newcomers from Iceland flying Ferry crews or replacements?"

"Mostly Ferry crews. But you can see, sir, that our crew position is better since those Category E's. And we've had twelve from Flak houses, eighteen from leave and sick, and twenty-eight new from Combat Crew Replacement Center today, sir."

The General nodded and concentrated now on the subtler revelations of the internal numbers. The board was much better than when he had gone to bed. Haley felt some of the pride in it that a modest wife knows in having made more than the most of her husband's limited provision. He knew perfectly well how the groups felt about his incessant phoning but the General expected high serviceability. He was frowning now.

"Why is the 641st slow again with Minor Repair, Haley?"

"That instrument man, sir. He was just a watchmaker, you know, a civilian. His work is good but he will fall asleep on his bench toward the end of the night."

Evans re-entered the room in time to hear the last of this and see the General nod quietly. It was not necessary for him to return while Haley was there but today his new curiosity had brought him back. He could see now that they were almost done with the recital.

"Fifty-eight crews then for fifty-three certain planes so far, not counting the Iceland bunch. Is all leave still canceled?"

"Yes, sir."

24

"And eleven crews graduate today?"

"If they get back, sir."

"We lose 'em anyway. Let's see, we put up a hundred and forty-four this morning . . ."

"Two were Category E, sir. Collisions. And three aborted, but two of them are promised in that fifty-three for tomorrow."

"Fifty-three and one thirty-nine is one ninety-two. What can you promise me for tomorrow?"

Haley looked blank. "I can't promise anything but that fifty-three until we get today's landing count and battle damage, sir. If you'd like a projection based on previous experience . . ."

"Never mind," said Dennis.

They both knew that previous experience was meaningless against today's target. That was where the projections, all the arithmetic for that matter, always collapsed. Dennis could and often did work the whole long equation in his head.

So many missions meant so many hits; so many tons on the ones that hit (an internal equation of planes sent and distance) meant such-and-such a density of destruction in so wide a radius. Such-and-such a destruction over so wide a radius meant so many weeks, or degrees, of deprivation to Germany of something y useful or x vital. The net result might be a pockmark for industrial court plaster; it might be a deep true split in the structure that time and more bombs could widen.

It was possible. It was why the Fifth Division, all the divisions, were here. Men could make the plan as Dennis had helped to do. They could be directed to execute it, as he was. They could measure resources and intentions for this execution, but they shared control of it with the weather and the Germans.

Dennis knew the phones in Berlin were hot this minute with orders for new concrete, steel, labor, machinery. Somewhere else in Germany (Intelligence now thought it was probably Potsdam) Galland was doing his own arithmetic. His was in fighters that took only one motor and one pilot apiece and had not a quarter of the bomber's vulnerable surface. And he always had at least six hours more to repair and redispose. In many ways Dennis envied him. On the other hand he never knew whether he'd have to fight on the morrow. Dennis did. He spoke now.

"Ted said 'Warm.' Make out leave passes for 10 per cent but hold 'em till we get a count. How do the boys feel?"

"They're too tired to feel, sir," said Haley.

The arithmetic was over and Haley knew they might as well not have done it. It was always meaningless until the landing count and battle damage from the day's mission were tabulated. But the General checked his board after every absence from the office. Only then would he take up the rest of his problems. Haley braced himself slightly.

"Well, what else?"

"Another rape case, I'm afraid, sir."

"Combat crew or base personnel?"

"A navigator, sir."

"Nuts. When's a navigator had time to get raped?"

Haley understood this to be partly jocular but it wasn't safe to joke until he got past the critical point of this case.

26

"Complaint was he did the raping. Last night, sir."

Evans was wondering how even a lieutenant could be stupid enough to get himself into trouble over something so simple. Navigators had flying pay and should have many accesses to whiskey. It was Evans's experience of women that even if you knocked 'em flat and forced 'em while they fluttered, a few drinks and a little patience afterwards left no problems worse than a return engagement. He noted with approval that the General was as skeptical as he was.

"A navigator raped somebody between yesterday's mission and today's? Who's complaining, the girl or her mother?"

"Her mother, sir. Mrs. Daphne Magruder, Tranquillity Cottage, the High Street, Undershot-Overhill."

Evans almost laughed aloud. There was a lieutenant for you. There wasn't an enlisted man on the station who couldn't have handled that pair. Most of them had. Astonishment betrayed him into an inadvertence.

"I know them people, sir."

"No doubt," said the General. But his mind was on Haley, who could now see the critical question coming. It came.

"Did our boy go there alone?"

"I'm afraid he did, sir."

"Damn it, Haley, I've told you before: when these boys tomcat they're to go in pairs. How can you expect one man, flying missions, to keep the whole family happy?"

Haley understood that the General's exasperation was directed not at him but at the essential stupidity of preventable trouble. He also knew that Dennis knew the

27

trouble was not really preventable. They might as well order men to catch cold two at a time.

"I'll have the order repeated, sir."

"Have you told the Judge Advocate?"

"Not yet, sir. We're bottlenecked on navigators and this man has ten missions left to go."

Evans had been thinking hard. The General was always fussy about his board but there had been a warning for the wary in the minuteness of this last examination. If he was going to send 'em three days running it would be hard to get off the station tonight.

"Excuse me, sir. Would the General like to square . . . that is, have this matter attended to by negotiation, sir?"

"Yes."

"If I could have an order on Mess Supply for two gallons of ice cream and a few hours off, sir . . ."

He let his voice trail off just short of a promise. The General looked at Haley, who considered and nodded slightly.

"Get it and get going."

"With the General's permission, sir, these matters are better attended to in the evening."

"All right. What else, Haley?"

Haley now produced the letter from the Society for the Preservation of Cultural and Artistic Treasures Against Vandalism. He had been severe with the clerk who had suggested replying in countercomplaint that such heavy embossed paper imperiled soldiers with piles. He knew, however, that Dennis would probably be severe with him about it, and though he extended the letter he summarized to save Dennis's time and temper.

"I'm afraid it *was* our Division hit that goddamned cathedral, sir. The man's changed his story. You remember, sir, first he said they were shot up and lost a motor and were straggling, so he salvoed into cloud to lighten ship?"

"They *were* shot up," Dennis remembered.

"Yes, sir. Next time out the man got hit. He's in the hospital now and says he wants to tell the truth. He says the war's made him an atheist and when he saw he couldn't reach the target with his bombs anyway he threw 'em into that cathedral just to show God what he thought of one of His lower echelons."

Dennis ignored the proffered letter. "Could he have got home with his bombs?"

Haley hesitated. Privately he thought the man should have but he was not being asked what he thought.

"He was deep in France on three motors, sir."

"Go to the hospital and chew his ass out," said Dennis. "Tell him for me we don't haul bombs through the sub belt to waste on atheism or any other religion. Then write the Society it was an emergency necessary to save life. Now, anything else?"

"Nothing of consequence, sir."

"Get the weatherman."

Haley called curtly through the Ops door and Major Belding Davis shuffled in, unmilitary, untidy, and unconcerned about it as always. He was a first-rate civilian meteorologist and he considered it the army's own fault to have put him in uniform. It had been done because the army feared civilians as it feared everything it could not regulate; the result was to make a bad officer out of a good scientist. Davis knew that he did not need regulation. He was conscientious and diligent. The uniform simply made him resentful and the rank made everyone under him resentful.

The one bright spot in the matter for him was that General Dennis seemed to understand this. His dealings with Davis were strictly professional and he paid no attention to anything else. Davis had learned to respect the General's knowledge of meteorology up to a point. Beyond that it was hopeless because the General was incurably subjective about weather. He thought, as most people did, only of its accommodation to his own purposes.

Davis was familiar, from civilian life, with this attitude, but the army had produced a variation on it that troubled him. Weather, for military understanding, was studied, estimated, and prophesied at two-hour intervals in each one of innumerable ascending headquarters from Operating Group to Hemisphere Commander.

The readings and estimates were made by different men, having access to different parts of the same available data; the prophesies reflected the many differences. At first Davis had thought this merely another instance of the superfluity and confusion of all things military. Lately he had begun to realize that as weather was a determinative factor in action, its readings fixed responsibility for ordering that action.

Davis now briefly explained the current readings, taking as always a grim satisfaction in the fact that even Army Regulations could not make nature disclose its intentions in the same forms to different men at two-hour intervals.

"General Kane's people refuse concurrence pending

further development, sir. But I think when I bring you the eighteen hundred map. . . ."

Today Dennis was unusually impatient. He strode to the masking curtain and pulled it back from the Operational map.

"Show me what *you* think on this map and keep your mouth shut about what you see," he said.

To orient himself, Davis studied the large, conventional 1 x 250,000 military map of England and Northern Europe. He had seldom seen this particular one on which targets were marked before attack. With a start he noted now a new little triangle of three black marks, deep in Germany. One of them had already been crossed through with savage red crayon on the plexiglass covering. It was yesterday's target; the inference was unmistakable. Humanly Davis had been irritated by his exclusion from any part in Plans except weather itself. He forgot himself in momentary astonishment at the location of those marks. Beside him Haley picked up a piece of red crayon and eyed one of them.

"Time for an improvement, isn't it, sir?"

"Improvement?" The General's mind was on weather.

"Colonel Martin said 'Primary plastered,' sir."

The crayon was touching the plexiglass when the General stopped Haley. He was smiling but his voice was firm.

"Let's let Ted do that."

"Of course, sir," said Haley apologetically.

Davis was ready now and began with an exposition of the prospects along the coastal fringe but Dennis stopped him short.

"Never mind the coastal fringe. What about here?"

31

His knuckles rapped the little triangle of black marks.

"My God, sir. Three days running in there?"

Too late, Davis remembered that he was not a part of Plans. The General did not raise his voice but it bit like a drill.

"Major, I'm consulting you about the weather."

Evans could feel his hackles rise at the General's tone and was glad those eyes were not on him. For Davis he felt no sympathy. He had sweated out too many of weather's mistakes to pity a fool who spoke out of turn about troubles that were not his. He saw Davis recoil a little, gather himself, and run through a rapid recital of the available facts and his opinion.

"I'm not sure Kane's people will agree, sir, but . . ."

"But you yourself think it will be all right in here?"

"Yes, sir."

"And over the bases for landing?"

"Yes, sir. I'm sure of that."

"Bring anything else as you get it."

Davis went out, disgruntled. Dennis turned on Haley, "Have *you* anything from Headquarters?"

This, Evans knew, also meant Kane's, which was the next step up in the progression. Previously Evans had thought of everything above the headquarters of his own squadron as one homogeneous malevolence. Now he realized that Dennis was talking about his boss, presumably the one who might fire him. Evans kept his ears tuned.

"They're releasing all divisions to commanders' discretion for tomorrow, sir. General Kane is reported so busy in that London conference that he will be unable to pass on the weather personally."

The Sergeant had a swift impression that Dennis and

Haley might have smiled at each other if Dennis had not suddenly glanced over to where he was standing quietly at ease.

"Any squawk from Washington yet?"

"Not yet, sir." This time they both smiled, as everyone did at mention of Washington, but the smiles were brief.

"Send Captain Jenks in."

"Want me with you, sir?"

"No. I'll try him alone again."

Evans thought Haley looked relieved, though faintly disapproving. But all the witnesses in the army wouldn't help that one. Evans scuttled toward the anteroom door, anxious to take delivery on his whiskey and eager to avoid Haley until the time when he could set out for the Magruders'. As he was going out he heard Dennis check Haley again at the door.

"Has that cable come for Ted?"

There were upwards of fifteen thousand men in the Division and every one of them felt a sense of personal concern over the kid Colonel Martin was sweating out. Prevailing opinion was that Mrs. Martin and the doctors were going to be seriously inconvenienced by the parachute; there were some, however, who said that they would never know what was happening until the new Martin phoned them that he had been forced down and was waiting in the nearest bar.

"No, sir," said Haley. "I've even checked with message center London. Mrs. Martin must be late."

"She's ten years late," said the General wearily.

Haley and Evans both hesitated until it was plain that he had not been talking to them. After a second they went out.

2

Alone, Dennis removed the coffee cup from his desk and threw the cigar into the stove. Then he sat down with the Jenks file before him but he did not open it. The roots of this case went to something deeper than that file. He was going to have to dig it out of the boy himself, if there were time, if he could.

Dennis had not wasted a second cursing the misfortune that had brought this up at the most critical juncture, so far, of the Fifth Division's war. These things always happened in armies sooner or later. This one had happened to the Fifth Division this morning. Dennis intended, if it were militarily possible, to keep it in the Division and save the boy. From the visible evidence it did not look possible.

Captain Jenks entered, marching correctly before a frightened guard. Dennis noted that the men in the guardhouse had been too literal about close arrest; they might have allowed Jenks to shave and change out of those flying coveralls. He returned the guard's salute, instructed him to wait outside, and studied Jenks narrowly through the brief interval of the guard's exit. The boy was scared but that young, rather strong face still had rigidity and restraint. No man flew nineteen missions without learning a lot about fear. This boy would still fight. Dennis took pains to make his voice as even as he could.

"Jenks, have you thought this over?"

"I thought it over this morning," said Jenks.

Dennis noticed the absence of any "sir." This boy knew he was beyond the help of manners.

"You've had more time."

"I don't need more time."

There was always the chance that a few hours of solitude would produce a change. Dennis had already risked eleven hours for the chance. Jenks knew as well as he did that there were only thirteen hours left but he had not changed.

"Damn it, boy, do you realize that this is serious?"

"Yes, for both of us."

"What are you hinting at?"

"I'm not getting killed to make you a record," said Jenks. "I'll tell the court so, too, and the whole damned world."

"What else will you tell them?"

"That you lost forty bombers, four hundred men, by deliberately sending us a hundred and sixty miles beyond fighter cover yesterday. This morning, when we're entitled to a milk run, you order us a hundred and eighty miles beyond the fighters."

"Why do you think you're entitled to a milk run?"

"After yesterday's losses? Besides, I can read a calendar."

Dennis knew now that the boy was going to fight to the end, as anyone would fight for his own life. He was working toward his one chance. Dennis couldn't tell yet whether it was transparency or purpose that had made him expose this chance a little, almost as if to show its strength. Under the letter of the law he was doomed and he was not going to fight the law. He was going to fight Dennis himself.

"What's the calendar got to do with it?"

"You big boys think flak fodder like us can't even read, don't you? Where does the Air Corps get all those lovely new statistical records for sorties and tonnages that General Kane announces every month? They get 'em on milk runs, the last three or four days."

"So you would have gone on an easy one today?"

"I'm entitled to it."

Inwardly Dennis was torn between immediate relief and a darkening sense of the ultimate hopelessness of this. There had been from the first the possibility that he was dealing with a sincere, stubborn, martyr. The boy might have been risking personal fate to lighten for the others the severity of their official sentence.

"Eleven other crews took this for their last mission."

"That's their business," said Jenks. "If you big shots are entitled to a record racket so am I."

His brief immediate relief faded into a heavier sadness. The contingency he had probed would have been troublesome; this was going to be tragic.

"Did it never occur to you, Jenks, that there might be another reason for these particular record missions?"

"What?"

"Destroying something that can kill a lot more than four hundred boys."

For the first time Jenks shifted uneasily on his feet.

"Everything in Germany is made to kill people. Why can't we hit targets under fighter cover like General Kane promised?"

"He didn't promise that."

Jenks hesitated. Dennis knew now that he was cracking the case the boy had worked out for himself in the guardhouse. Jenks made a further effort to sound reasonable, persuasive.

"Well, everyone who knows the army knew what General Kane meant in the press interview after that rat race over Bremfurt six weeks ago. That day we lost nineteen and the whole Air Corps turned itself inside out explaining. Yesterday we lost forty and today will be worse . . ." Jenks hesitated. Then, as if realizing the irrelevance of all this, he lowered his voice insinuatingly.

"How do you think the public is going to like this?"

Dennis had to fight down that feeling in the pit of his stomach. They were coming to the end of it. Possibly the boy's corruption did derive from the prevarications of the army's press and public relations policy. But Dennis had to deal with his behavior. He spoke curtly.

"The public isn't my business."

Jenks misread his short silence for intimidation.

"What would the press say if they knew you ordered both these attacks on your own authority when General Kane was absent from weather conferences at his headquarters?"

"That isn't your business. You were ordered to go. After learning the target you refused."

He saw Jenks stiffen under the gaff of the stripped, naked truth and then slowly go limp. His voice became defensive.

"I've been to plenty tough targets."

Dennis tapped the file. "You aborted from the two toughest missions prior to yesterday."

"For mechanical malfunctions." Jenks was breathing hard.

"One engineer's examination said: 'Possibly justifiable.' The other one said: 'Defect not discernible.' "

"It was plenty discernible to me . . . and my copilot will tell you the same thing, unless he's prejudiced."

"He should be. He's flying your seat today. And you're a Squadron Commander with a D.F.C. That just makes it worse."

"For somebody," said Jenks, but it was only an echo of bravado. Dennis had shattered him purposely to make him see the hopelessness of his case, to find, if it were humanly possible, some reason for this in the wreckage.

Dennis had thought himself familiar with every form of fear. He had seen them all, from the strait-jacket cases to the ones who simply sat alone, in lounge and bar and mess, waiting consciously for the inevitable moment when their own paralyzed reflexes would give them final release. He still did not think this was simple fear. He had not thought so from the first. Something was eluding him here as it would elude the court. No court would even bother to search behind such utterly damning facts. And yet the man had flown nineteen missions. Wearily, Dennis began again.

"Jenks, if you've got any legitimate reason whatever . . ."

The anteroom door crashed open and the General looked up with impatience to see Evans holding it ajar. Even before he could voice a rebuke the Sergeant spoke warningly.

"Major General R. G. Kane and party, sir."

38

Chapter Three

GENERAL KANE seldom visited the operating echelons of his command. He would have considered any need to do so a symptom of weakness in the subordinate commander involved, a condition remediable by instant replacement. Instead he ruled with painstaking attention from desk and telephone. Like every commander he bridged a gulf between upper and nether regions, connecting and explaining them to each other. Policy and Plans came down: results went up. His duty was to execute the former and answer for the latter.

Officially his status between the worlds he linked was rigidly neutral. But no man became a major general without realizing that the practical division of his two worlds was simple. Below him were troubles, above him opportunities.

Kane had moved upward through life because his eyes were fixed upward. But they had never been blind to the fact that men must climb on something solid. He had always fought fiercely, on his own level and above it, for the subordinates he wanted. When he got them he made it his business to see that they liked working for him.

This transitory war with Germany had not changed either Kane or the conditions of life that had made him. It had only expanded both his troubles and his opportunities. He remained vigilant of his key subordinates, who, sharing in the bonanza that had elevated him, were now mostly brigadiers.

But the lieutenant generals, the admirals, the Embassy, the press, the Prime Minister, and Kane's Allied opposite numbers were in London. There the battle lines of the permanent wars, between the army and the navy, between the army and its troublesome stepson of the air, between service and civilians, had been extended from Washington. And there, for most of every day and late into the night, Kane fought the wars he knew best.

The luxury of liking or disliking people he had long since abandoned as an extravagance beyond the military life. But he had deliberately incurred the wrath of three lieutenant generals to get Dennis for himself.

Dennis could not only operate a division, he could have operated an air army. He was young but so was the war. There were men with three stars who would have traded records with him. Kane had spent long hours with his most private card index before making the decision. It was finally his conclusion that of all the coming men in the army he wanted firmly placed before turning his back on the fickleness of Washington, Dennis was foremost.

Professionally it had been a hard decision. Final choice had lain between Dennis and Garnett, who had been strongly urged upon him. The two men were opposites. Garnett's very real talent for staff work and planning had taken him indoors to fight the navy and Congress, while Dennis, by preference, was still flying and commanding small echelons. Among the other factors, Kane had had to weigh operational against diplomatic capability.

Earlier in his own career Kane had had to make the same essential choice for himself. He had judged that the future lay inside. He had lived through the bitterness of seeing some of the men who stayed out of doors appointed to superior commands which he himself had blueprinted. The lesson had not escaped him, nor had the fact that Garnett was urged upon him and Dennis stubbornly denied him.

He had taken Dennis, and the victory of getting him, as proof of his own power at first. But with Garnett's consolatory appointment to the Secretaryship of the United Chiefs of Staff the decision had returned to haunt Kane. Confirmation that he was big enough to demand, and get, Dennis had automatically reduced Dennis in his eyes.

For Dennis never would have taken the job with the United Chiefs anyway, and but for Kane's own choice would by now probably have been safely sidetracked in the Pacific. Whereas Garnett, in the Pentagon, and conscious of Kane's known refusal of him, was dangerous. His sudden arrival in London on business that Kane instantly recognized as insufficient for an emissary of such weight had given Kane considerable anxiety.

Dennis, jumping to attention at Evans's announcement, saw instantly that Kane was worried about something. He carried his hard, spare figure more jauntily than ever. The ruddy face under the jet-black hair was frozen in the fixed, unnatural smile which the army had once used to adorn recruiting posters. His air of affable, almost exuberant cordiality would have persuaded any stranger, as it was worn to persuade Dennis, that he hadn't a care in the world. Not until he saw Garnett step through the door after Kane did Dennis understand.

"I'm very sorry, sir," he said. "If I'd known you were visiting us I'd have been at the gate."

"Don't speak of it, Casey, don't speak of it. Cliff Garnett here wanted to see a real operational headquarters at work so I brought him straight down from London without waiting on protocol. You remember Cliff, of course?"

At another time Dennis might have laughed. Every regular in the army knew that Garnett was the fifth successive General Officer of his name. The Garnett legend had begun at Chapultepec. He and Dennis had been classmates. They had worked together as young men and, with their brides, lived across the fences from each other in the dismal family quarters at Hawaii, in the Philippines, in the Canal Zone. They had run neck and neck for the first silver bar in the class. Dennis had got it. Later they had drifted apart a little. But within the narrow confines of the Corps itself they had remained as aware of each other as vice-presidents in a small firm. Garnett had got his star first but Dennis had the Fifth Division. At least, he reflected, he had had it until now.

"Hello, Casey. You fellows are certainly doing a wonderful job over here."

He muttered something which he hoped sounded satisfactorily responsive and studied Garnett himself. The Pentagon had washed away the deep tan that had always been Garnett's peacetime pride. Once he had been assiduous about exercise; now his tailor would have been shocked at the tightness of that excellent uniform. He

42

was not yet fat, but desk work and deprivation of exercise showed quickly on him. Dennis noted with amusement that he had already managed to procure one of the little British sword canes which so delighted some American generals in London. Then with a start Dennis realized he'd been away from the higher echelons too long. Garnett hadn't had time to procure that toy: Kane had given it to him.

But Kane was now ostentatiously introducing him to a major whom the General presented as his new aide. The handshake was too firm; the face and eyes had already taken on the unctuous familiarity of the job.

"I'm very happy to meet the commander of our famous Fifth Division," said Major Prescott.

"Have you replaced Major Tailor?"

"For the moment, anyway, sir," said Prescott. "He went home to do a book and movie on General . . . that is, on this Air Army, so I'm sort of taking over."

"And here, Casey," said Kane, "is my friend Elmer Brockhurst."

Dennis had been too intent on Garnett to notice that the correspondent had entered, chatting familiarly with Prescott, and now confronted him with an outstretched hand below his faint smile. Dennis ignored the hand.

"General Kane, I've refused this man the station for worming operational information out of my people."

He saw anger flash and then fade, deep under Kane's blank simulation of a smile.

"Now, my boy, that's one of the things I've come down here about. You and Brockie were both trying to do right and . . ."

He had been looking about the room as he spoke and

his eyes had fallen for the first time on Captain Jenks, waiting at rigid attention. With instant decision Kane left the Brockhurst matter in the silent air which he had known to close over hotter issues than this, and making straight for the Captain he extended a hand, face and voice exuding paternal cordiality.

"Why, Captain Jenks, delighted to see you, my boy."

Brockhurst watched Dennis almost visibly frosting over as Kane shook hands with the Captain and then, throwing an affectionate arm around his dirty coveralls, led him back to General Garnett.

"Cliff, this is one of our real heroes. I had the pleasure of decorating him with the D.F.C. while Casey was in the hospital a while ago. He's a Squadron Commander and already has sixteen missions. It is sixteen, isn't it, Captain?"

"Nineteen now, sir." Jenks was embarrassed but he was visibly absorbing assurance from General Kane's patronage.

"Nineteen, eh," chuckled Kane. "I guess that name on your ship hardly applies any more. Captain Jenks named his Fortress the *Urgent Virgin*, Cliff. Maybe you saw her. Elmer here got us a wonderful spread on her in *Coverage*—three pages and nine pictures."

Brockhurst now realized that this was indeed the boy on whom he had done the special article. He had begun the assignment with zest and ended it holding his nose. In twelve years of newspaper work he had never seen anyone, from actresses to presidents, as camera conscious as that kid.

At the time he had shrugged and blamed the uniform. Since then he had begun to wonder. The effect of the uniform was illusory; it only intensified what was in the man. Kane's cunning and Dennis's inhuman austerity seemed sound examples. He attuned his ears as Kane went on.

"What brings you up to Division Headquarters today, my boy? Are you helping General Dennis here?"

Jenks hesitated: "Not exactly, sir."

"It's a disciplinary matter, sir," said Dennis. "Captain Jenks and I will attend to it later."

He indicated the door to Jenks, but Kane did not remove the firm arm around the Captain's shoulder.

"This is what you wanted to see, Cliff, real field problems. Now Casey, you and Captain Jenks carry right on just as if we weren't here. If there's one thing I pride myself on it's not interfering with the vital work of my divisions."

Dennis looked pointedly from Kane to Brockhurst.

"This is not a matter for the press, sir."

Evans, watching intently from his post by the door, scowled to himself. Garnett looked like one of the finicky ones to him, and if Dennis were trying to get himself fired he could not have chosen a better way. Kane's courtship of the press was as notorious throughout the Division as in the Savoy. Evans saw him flush angrily before he addressed Dennis.

"Brockie is a friend of mine, General." He let this sink in before turning his affability on Jenks again.

"Well, what's the disciplinary trouble, my boy? Some of those high-spirited young pilots of yours getting out of hand?"

Jenks shuffled his foot through a perceptible silence.

"Perhaps General Dennis will explain, sir."

"Captain Jenks is under arrest for refusal to fly the mission as ordered this morning, sir," said Dennis.

2

Dennis had hoped to spare his visitors the pain of the preliminaries in the Jenks case. It would be bad enough for Kane if and when it got up to his level. To have it aired, prematurely, before the press and a visitor, especially a visitor of Garnett's level, shocked his entire training. He could see that Kane, too late, felt the same way. The truth had hit him like a quirt. He reddened and removed his arm hastily from Jenks's shoulder before regarding the Captain with reproachful appeal.

"My boy . . . Captain Jenks . . . I don't believe it."

Of all of them Jenks had had the most preparation. He had known it would have to come out, whether here or later. He spoke quietly, managing an air of patient grievance.

"It's true, sir, as far as the General went." Then, boldly, he counterattacked. "Do you know what the target was, General Kane?"

Kane palpably did not. Caught squarely he hesitated and then turned on Brockhurst, his voice weighted with gravity.

"Brockie, I'm afraid there *is* a question of military security if you don't mind . . ."

Brockhurst did mind, acutely, but he knew that he could get what he wanted when he had Kane alone. He lingered just long enough to let Kane feel his displeasure

46

and then walked out the anteroom door. As it closed
behind him Dennis tried swiftly to cover for Kane,
though he well knew that Garnett would not have
missed the effect of the Captain's question. The boy
was shrewd; he was going to make the maximum trouble.

"The target was Schweinhafen, sir," said Dennis.

"*Schweinhafen!* You've begun Operation Stitch?"

This was worse and worse. Inwardly Dennis now
cursed Jenks for the first time. It was shocking to have
Kane in such a position before Garnett, but there was no
help for it.

"Began yesterday with Posenleben, sir."

"POSENLEBEN!" This time they could all see Kane
wilt a little under the third blow. "What happened?"

"Excellent results, sir. Over three-quarters total destruction and . . ."

"I mean what did you lose?"

"Forty, sir."

"*Forty!* Good God! Does the press know it?"

"They haven't released it, sir. I put a security blackout
on the whole thing as we agreed."

"Well, that's something." He had completely forgotten the presence of Jenks and was slowly regaining some
of his composure when the horror of the next thought
struck him.

"You didn't signal Washington, did you?"

This time Dennis had to check his own indignation
before speaking.

"Of course not, sir. Routine report to your headquarters only."

Kane knew they were all studying his agitation now
but he had no energy to waste on appearances. As al-

47

ways in crisis he was sorting out the ramifications of the problem in the order of their urgency and importance. Washington was the thing that could not wait. Next he would have to prepare to handle the press. After that would be time enough to hush up the Jenks matter and make whatever explanations might be necessary to Garnett and Dennis.

"Were the claims high, Casey?"

"Very, sir. I was too busy with bomb damage assessment to count them myself but . . ."

"Have them tabulated at once, by groups, on heavy board, ready to photograph."

While Dennis was transmitting the order into the Ops room Kane thought rapidly but he knew he was not thinking clearly. There were so many sides to this mess. Jenks, the operation, the press, Washington, Garnett — each place his mind touched seemed hotter. The difficulty fired in him a surging wrath at the injustice of it. No man alive worked harder than he did; this kind of luck haunted him, every stroke of it compounding every other one. He could see that he was going to have to stop and explain to Garnett as he went along. It was unsafe not to. Garnett was already firing his first question at the returning Dennis.

"Would someone mind explaining to a visitor what this Operation Stitch is?"

Dennis hesitated appropriately and then, as Kane kept his abstracted silence, spoke briefly.

"Kind of a three-horse parlay, Cliff. Posenleben, Schweinhafen, and" — he glanced pointedly at Jenks and Prescott — "one other."

"I thought I was reasonably familiar with your directive," said Garnett. "But I don't remember those."

Kane still ignored it. Dennis spoke dryly.

"Some things aren't in directives, Cliff."

"Evidently." Garnett turned squarely to Kane. "I'm surprised that the United Chiefs haven't been informed of this, General Kane."

Evans, listening delightedly behind his impassivity, had difficulty in suppressing a start. That guy might look like an actor but nobody spoke to major generals that way by accident. Locking his face muscles he waited for Kane to blast the Brigadier out of the room. Kane turned to Garnett with a rueful, disarming smile.

"I was going to send them a provisional plan but I didn't know General Dennis intended implementing it so soon."

Evans saw Dennis stiffen and saw the color change under the thin blond hair at the back of his neck. But it was the Major with the face like a toad's belly who spoke, ingratiatingly, to Garnett.

"The whole idea was General Dennis's, sir."

"And I'll explain it myself, Major," said Dennis abrasively. "General Kane, do you wish to detain Captain Jenks further, sir?"

Kane wished that Captain Jenks had been stillborn. He had just begun to figure out the line for Washington and the press when this was thrust back into his face. But Garnett was watching this, too, closely.

"Did you go on the mission yesterday, Jenks?"

"I did. It was a bloody massacre. Today will be worse."

With a spasm Kane realized that this was probably true.

"Any news from today, General Dennis?"

"Strike signal from Colonel Martin, sir. It said: 'Primary plastered.' "

"I mean about losses."

"Ted indicated fighting. No details yet, sir."

Unexpectedly Evans now saw Garnett wheel on Dennis.

"So Ted is flying missions?"

"He led the Division today. Yesterday too."

He knew only too well what was coming. Garnett's sister was married, unhappily, to Ted Martin. Dennis had been Martin's best man. No matter how scrupulously everyone behaved, the alignment of sympathies was obvious. Garnett, with good reason, worried about the marriage. Dennis hated being dragged into it. But now that Prescott had pulled Kane a little to one side for some detailed reminder Dennis could see Garnett gathering himself for the chance.

"You know about Helen, of course, Casey?"

"Sure. Any news yet?"

"Not when I left but she's due any minute. Ted shouldn't be flying missions at all, let alone just now."

He knew that Garnett himself knew better than this. Yet he couldn't help resenting the intimation that he himself had not thought of that. He spoke more curtly than he intended.

"He gets paid to. General Kane, have you any further need of Captain Jenks?"

Whatever Prescott had whispered to Kane had restored his composure somewhat. He was speaking again to Jenks and with more confidence.

"And after the terrible strain of yesterday you felt

unable to take the responsibility of flying a crew again . . . you were under shock?"

Jenks got it instantly. "We were all under shock, sir. Two days running beyond fighter cover when you had practically promised us . . ."

"That's not exactly what I said."

Jenks checked quickly. "Well, sir, we all knew *you'd* never ask a thing like that, just to make a record. When we learned you'd released the Division to General Dennis and then this came up everyone was shocked."

"Everyone else went," said Dennis.

Kane cleared his throat. "General," he said, "as you know I pride myself on never interfering with the functioning of my subordinate echelons. But in a matter that touches one of our combat boys I know you will forgive an older commander's concern. With your permission I should like to talk to Captain Jenks alone."

Dennis dismissed Evans and invited Garnett and Prescott into the Ops room with him, but Kane stopped them. He himself would go into the anteroom with Jenks.

"That civilian's out there, sir," said Dennis.

Kane's voice was tart. "Brockie is my friend, General, and he has a very long head."

He led Jenks to the anteroom and, with an afterthought, beckoned Prescott to follow them. Dennis shrugged. There was no help for it. He tried to make himself smile cordially as he faced Garnett and waited for some more dirty linen.

Garnett, however, had understood his earlier rebuke. On everything except this lamentable family trouble he was a man of delicacy and perception. Recovering his normal urbanity now, he opened with some remarks about Dennis's own family. He had made a point of calling on them the day before he left. It was a normal courtesy but it was the kind many men overlooked. His consideration and the fresh letters he now delivered disarmed Dennis.

"They're fine, Casey, fine, and terribly proud of you."

Dennis judged that Garnett might be using this as a cover for whatever official business had brought him over, but he was grateful for the chance to forget official business momentarily. The thought of Cathy and his children, especially in such inevitable contrast to poor Ted's troubles, took him for a minute out of that bleak room. He asked some further questions and warmed himself in Garnett's ringing reassurances. It was decent of Cliff to have driven way out into Maryland in all the haste and turmoil of his departure. And Cliff genuinely did like his family.

"Lucy carries a picture of you in a cellophane case she made herself, Casey."

"Yeah?" He was embarrassed but greedy, too. "How's the kid?"

Garnett smiled. "Young William Mitchell gave me special orders. You're to destroy all of Germany except one little piece which he wants saved for his first bomb. He means it, too, Casey. He asked me if I thought you could do it."

Dennis could feel the very thought of that freckle-faced bundle of trouble renewing him. But he could no more share with Cliff than he could with anyone except Cathy the way he felt about his kids. He tried to make himself sound impersonal.

"What did you tell him?"

"Well, I told him with war you never know."

It was a typically guarded Garnett answer but it shattered the serenity Dennis had momentarily regained. Every time Ted took the Division he reminded himself sternly that it wasn't as bad as if young William Mitchell were doing it, but the margin was too thin for comfort. He spoke almost to reassure himself.

"Seven and a half years would be pretty bad even for the United Chiefs, Cliff."

Garnett tensed a little. "Don't be bitter, Casey. They have their troubles, too."

Then, sensing Dennis's instant contrition, he moved immediately to the inevitable topic.

"Helen is worried about Ted, Casey."

"Is she?"

"Very. You know that always was the real trouble."

"Was it?"

"Yes. In the early days, especially when you and Ted were testing, she got so she couldn't even answer the phone. That was why she wouldn't have kids then. She had no security, even for a day ahead."

He knew that Garnett realized as well as he did that none of the other girls had had any more security. It was the thing that made him so sensitive about it, so desperate to change it somehow, by talk. But it was past the help of talk and Dennis wanted only to drop the whole subject.

"No?"

"Oh, I know she left him, Casey, but think of her side of it. . . ."

*   *   *

Dennis had known from the first that he would never be able to think of her side of it fairly. He had known Helen Garnett since the days when she used to come to Academy Hops. The Garnett size and looks had been designed for men but Helen had the carriage for them and the Garnett habit of authority. Dennis danced with her punctiliously, once at each Hop, as he did with most of the sisters of his classmates. In those days neither Helen nor Cliff encouraged intimacy from Middle Westerners and Dennis did not regret it.

Thereafter he had seen more of her, at closer quarters, on her occasional visits to outlying posts. Dennis and Cathy both liked Cliff's wife, Natalie; army life forced propinquity upon them and they had exchanged dinners, played cards, alternated in the hospitality of the weekly movies, and loaned and borrowed food and bathtub gin on a dozen dreary fields from Clark to Bolling. Helen's visits always touched these exiles, for the girls at least, with the fleeting metropolitan glamour of new clothes and hair styles. To the married men she brought the Washington gossip, shrewdly assessed and evaluated by the insight of three generations of family table talk on military politics.

To the young bachelor officers who thronged the houses during her visits she brought the gaiety of visiting royalty, brief, bright dreams of a powerful connection and an expert facility for terminating these hopes without undue pain. Even they seemed to understand and approve the Garnetts' tacit assumption that Helen belonged to a brighter world than the services offered. For all of his normal acuteness Dennis had been a little surprised the first time Cathy had privately pronounced her cold-blooded.

In time the Garnetts and Dennises drifted apart to different posts on different assignment. It was following one of these separations that the Dennises had been ordered, as unexpectedly and inconveniently as always, to Washington during the summer while Cathy was having William Mitchell. The orders were only temporary and had caught them in what was even for them a financial crisis. The sweltering, cockroach-ridden little flat on H Street was one of their few unhappy memories.

By then Ted Martin had become practically a member of the family. With the relative opulence of a bachelor on flying pay he had his own flat in Georgetown, a new car, and an expanding address book which did not run to dowagers. He had come over to the Dennis flat one Sunday with an offer to drive them out of the city heat for dinner just as Cliff was telephoning to ask them across the river for a julep. Cliff had cordially included him in the invitation.

Two of the previous Generals Garnett had married prudently.

While Garnett's Tree was not a mansion the big hall was cool with the river breeze coming in across the terrace and the old Georgian brick wore the languorous charm of its generations with shabby grace. They had stepped from dazzling sunlight on the bluestone drive into a serene antiquity, just as Helen burst into the opposite terrace door, her black hair vivid against a summery white dress.

She had greeted Cathy and Dennis warmly enough but with the slight inattentiveness she always accorded married people. She had been turning away from her introduction to Ted before the echo of his name caught in her consciousness and she had repeated, as people had begun to repeat that name:

"Not *the* Lieutenant Martin . . . ? Why, Cliff never told me he knew you."

On the terrace Cliff had introduced them with evident satisfaction to Helen's fiancé, a prosperous-looking middle-aged stockbroker who sighed amiably over his julep.

"You fellows have all the fun. What are you two going to do next, Captain Dennis?"

They had spent a pleasant afternoon over Cliff's excellent juleps and departed over Helen's vociferous insistence that they remain for pickup supper. On the way down the river Cathy had kidded Ted about Helen's obvious interest in him. Ted had replied indifferently that the brassière had not yet been made which could keep her from being anything but another Garnett stuffed shirt.

The next morning Helen had called Cathy to ask for Ted's address and phone number. It happened that that week he had been flying something to Sacramento. In the eight days of his absence Helen had called Cathy, three times more.

Ted had been back about six weeks when Garnett came out from the War Department to the hangar one morning to ask Dennis bluntly what he knew about this Lieutenant Martin. The question had astonished Dennis. He had begun to explain what he had very early perceived and now the whole service, in fact the whole country, was beginning to realize about Lieutenant Martin when Garnett cut him short impatiently.

"I know all that. Casey, Helen's broken her engagement to Morton Collins."

The connection seemed to him incredible. Ted had not mentioned Helen since that Sunday. He told him this but Garnett only shook his head and then blurted: —

"It's not as if he'd been at the Point with us. Does he understand *all* the rules, Casey?"

All the rules meant the unwritten but explicit one that propinquity and boredom had established to protect peacetime tedium: all the brothers were valiant, all the sisters were virtuous. The equally explicit corollary to this rule was that all exceptions to it must be conducted three miles from the flagpole.

He had reassured Garnett as delicately as he could. He knew that Cliff's judgments were apt to be superficial and in this case probably not untinged with envy. Even by then the experts were trying to dismiss the foundations of the growing Martin legend with the simple explanation of Martin luck. Dennis knew better. There was far more than luck in the perfection of that flying, far more than an aviator in the complexity of the man himself.

Women generally apprehended this more quickly than men. Even as an obscure youngster Martin had always had a wide choice of diversion and had accepted it with the casual, detached amusement he seemed to accord everything except flying itself. Yet Dennis doubted that any woman had ever touched the capacity for thought and feeling locked up in the pilot below

57

the troublesome and insubordinate young lieutenant. He could scarcely tell Cliff that Helen seemed the last woman in the world to do it. He could and did tell him privately that he knew Ted was happily preoccupied in half a dozen other directions.

Garnett had thanked him and gone off glumly. Dennis had forgotten it until in the privacy of their bedroom that night Cathy had remarked that they saw little of Ted lately. She had looked around from her hair combing indignantly as he told her of Cliff's visit that day.

"Ted indeed! Why doesn't he teach Helen the rules?"

"Helen?"

"Casey! She had rape in her eye that afternoon."

He had protested, more to himself than to her; in the first place he didn't believe it. If it were true, Ted had survived other encounters with that peril.

"No wonder you two can fly blind! Don't you realize she's playing for keeps?"

"Well, I don't know what we can do . . . Ted's of age . . ."

"And she's three years older. Casey, can't you order him somewhere?"

He had explained to her that newly created captains did not order people anywhere. Later in the week they accepted a hasty dinner invitation from the Garnetts with foreboding. Ted's car was in the driveway as they arrived. In the hall Ted and Helen greeted them arm in arm, Ted's face stiff with an unnatural smile as Helen announced the engagement to them.

The trouble came fast. Three months later Ted had driven into the hangar and the first sight of him told

58

Dennis that he was unfit to fly. Instead of pretending he had beckoned Dennis into the car and slammed the door for privacy.

"Casey, is there any station where officers can't take wives?"

Dennis had known by then, they had all known, that it was going badly. The finality of this shocked him. It was the first time Ted had spoken of it to him and he fell back on their old habits; they did not beat around the bush with each other.

"Look, Ted; these things adjust themselves in time. And you've got the kid to think of . . ."

"There isn't any kid," said Ted. "There never was."

With an effort he pulled his attention back to Garnett, who was still talking.

". . . five years in boardinghouses on gold-bar pay . . . the morning he made first he had to call his C.O. a goddamned fool to his face and get busted before lunch. That afternoon he turned down twelve thousand a year from the best airline in America. What would you have thought?"

It was like an old, old record caught in one groove, repeating again and again a fragment of an unhappy tune. He didn't mean to sound unsympathetic but what was there to say?

"I've always thought he was a rare guy, Cliff."

"She's realized that, Casey. She did go back to him."

"Cliff, what's all this leading to?"

"Does Ted think she just came back to him and is having that kid because he is pretty secure now?"

"You'll have to ask Ted what he thinks. It's his business."

"Ted and I were never very close," persisted Garnett. "You know what he thinks of you."

"Maybe that's because I don't try to run his life."

"It's in your hands. You don't have to send him at his age."

Dennis flinched and looked at his wrist watch.

"I don't have to send any of them. We could all be secure, under Hitler."

Instantly he felt ashamed of the retort because he knew that Garnett, too, was deeply troubled. But there was no time for this kind of trouble now. He was relieved at the sight of Kane leading his party into the room again, walking with some of his old assurance as he brought Jenks straight over to them.

"General Dennis, Captain Jenks is obviously the victim of a shock condition induced by the strain of his nineteen missions. This is a clear-cut case of combat fatigue, a medical, not a disciplinary, matter. He needs immediate rest."

"Sir, did the Captain tell you that he finished ten days in a rest house Thursday and has been medically certified fit for the completion of this tour?"

He saw Kane coloring again, apoplectically, but it did not cool his own fury. This preposterous fabrication was an insult to his investigation. It was probably the idea of Prescott, whose smirk had vanished now. Kane, with a clear head, would never have fallen for such a stupid stratagem. Already he had begun to think of a new way out but Prescott, now under a heightened obligation, spoke first.

"Captain Jenks, did you know of any defect in your

plane that would have made such a long flight impossible for it?"

"His copilot took the plane. It hasn't aborted." Dennis chopped the words out fast to save Kane from this second, transparent trap. But although he had heard clearly, Kane clutched at the straw.

"We won't know that till the plane comes back," he said.

"If it comes back," said Dennis. He had never seen Kane fumble like this before. There must be serious trouble in London or Washington. Dennis felt doubly guilty that his chief should have to be worried with such a business at the moment. But Kane was regaining a little of his old brusqueness.

"We'll continue the investigation later, General," he said.

The guard answered Dennis instantly and they watched through a taut silence while he marched Jenks out.

"General," said Kane as the door closed, "this is very serious."

"Every detail will be checked, sir. It happened at five-twenty this morning. I've got the rest of the twenty-four hours."

He wanted to shield Kane from it as long as possible, to make him see that it was not his burden yet, that every resource would be strained to keep it from becoming his burden. But Kane's perceptions had outraced intermediate consolation.

"Twenty-four hours for what?"

"To charge him, sir." If Kane wanted to face it that was it.

"What charge are you considering?"

"Unless something new comes up the only possible charge is 'Desertion in the Face of the Enemy.'"

"Good God, boy! We can't shoot a man with nineteen missions and a D.F.C."

Dennis knew. His own mind had recoiled from the implication of this case. But it was out now.

"Do you think we'll ever have another tough mission if we don't, sir? At a group briefing this morning when the target map was uncovered I saw five men cross themselves. One fainted. But they went and they know Jenks didn't."

He could tell that Kane understood. It simply took time for any mind to face it. Garnett had already taken it in and was digesting it slowly. It was that presumptuous new aide who seemed to feel that speech, any speech, was better than what they were all thinking.

"Couldn't a quiet transfer be arranged, say to transport or training?" he asked.

"So he could go yellow there and kill passengers or students?"

But Prescott either didn't want to learn or couldn't.

"Precautions can be taken, General," he persisted. "There is such a thing as the end justifying the means. This case would put the honor of the whole Air Forces at stake."

"It already has. Every man in the Division knows it."

"I was thinking of the larger picture."

"You can. I'm thinking of the Division. It doesn't require your assistance, Major."

He did not enjoy squelching this worm but Prescott was going to embarrass General Kane with his effrontery sooner or later unless he learned some manners somewhere. Kane himself seemed to be catching up to this now.

"Homer, go talk this over, very thoroughly, with Elmer Brockhurst."

As the aide closed the anteroom door behind him Kane spoke a little apologetically to Dennis.

"Brockhurst has a remarkable feel for public reaction, Casey. We've got to consider every angle of this."

Dennis picked up the file and extended it to Kane.

"There are dubious engineers' reports on two previous abortions, sir. He apparently got this D.F.C. for happening to be in the lead and bringing a squadron home after the commander had gone down over Brest. But that's routine. He was made Squadron Commander after his twelfth mission, which is pretty fast for a boy with one questionable abortion at the time, even in a squadron with 72 per cent losses."

Kane did not take the file. He had not been paying full attention through the recital and his next question shocked Dennis.

"Have you talked to his Group Commander, Casey?"

"You didn't get yesterday's reports, sir?"

"No. I was at a meeting in London. Why?"

"Colonel Ledgrave went down yesterday, sir."

He could see both Kane and Garnett recoil from the news as he had done when he took it over the phone.

"My God," said Kane softly. "Leddy . . . any parachutes seen?"

"Two, coming out of the left waistgate, sir. But Leddy was riding with the bombardier and she exploded just as the waist gunners got out."

"Casey," said Garnett, "is it necessary for . . . for our own people . . . to go so often?"

"Yes."

Kane spoke again now, wearily but clearly.

"Had Leddy never mentioned Jenks to you?"

"Never, sir."

"That's my oversight, Casey. I had meant to tell you as I told him, in confidence, that Captain Jenks's uncle is on the Military Affairs Committee in the House."

3

Colonel Haley was not the most perceptive of men but entering just then he could feel the surcharged tension in the room. Garnett and Kane were looking at each other tensely. Dennis was nodding his head slowly over the Jenks file.

He noted that they all looked toward his entrance with a sense of relief for its distraction and he regretted that his errand would add to Dennis's immediate worries. He would have preferred to report directly to Kane as ranking officer in the room. Haley did not agree with the new regulations on the Visits of Officers from Higher Echelons. He had made a note to write the Adjutant General a strong recommendation for change when there was time, after the war, to get things decently straightened out again. Meanwhile the rules were clear, albeit improper in his view. Ignoring the others he addressed himself to Dennis.

"Two sightings, sir. First from the Royal Observer Corps. Thirty-nine coming over the Channel now."

"How did they look?"

"Ragged, sir. Five feathered props reported."

"What's the other?"

"Two in the Channel, so far, sir. Air Sea Rescue has a good plot on one and Spitfires will cover the pick-up."

Dennis nodded. Haley did his most formal about-face and closed the door quickly behind him.

"How soon will you have a count?" asked Kane.

"About forty minutes, sir. They'll start landing soon."

Kane nodded and stepped over to the window for a look at the sky. There was tarnish on the old-style wings he wore but he always forbade his sergeant to polish them.

"Am I right in surmising this sounds bad?" asked Garnett.

"Ted says they plastered the target."

"I was thinking about losses."

"That's one way of thinking of it," said Dennis shortly.

"Casey, what are you trying to do that's more important than losses? I'm very familiar with your directive and *this is* your build-up period. Frankly, I don't know what the United Chiefs will think."

"When did they start thinking?"

"Casey!" Kane had turned now to regard him sternly.

"Sorry, sir."

He knew he had that one coming. Kane seldom bothered to rebuke trifles. Now, as if regretting this, he came over to them and made his voice conciliatory.

"Casey, Cliff here has been sent over with some pretty important dope for us. I think I'll ask him to tell you the story just as he told it to me."

65

Dennis composed himself patiently, wondering which of Washington's multitudinous apprehensions had catapulted his classmate across the Atlantic. He could still remember the solemn minions who had flown in by highest priority to insist that the "nipples and other anatomical portions normally covered" of the young ladies painted on Fortress noses be overpainted with clothing.

Garnett appeared to have sensed his boredom. Instead of opening immediately he digressed for a short demonstration of the strength he represented.

"I'll tell Casey, of course, sir. But before I do I would like to be briefed on this Operation Stitch."

"Haven't you told him, sir?"

Kane thought before answering. "I thought it would be fairer for you to, since it's so largely your idea, Casey."

The disavowal was so obvious that it startled Dennis. He decided that he must be touchy today as he always was when Ted was out. The hell with it. He strode over to the Swastika on the wall and tapped it.

"Six weeks ago a German fighter, the one this came from, landed on the Number One Strip out there." He pointed and Cliff glanced briefly through the window.

"Shot up?"

"No. The pilot was a Czechoslovakian engineer and test pilot. He'd been forced to work for them but when they sent him to the Baltic with this job for testing he flew it here instead. The weather was ten tenths and this was the first field he saw when he broke through."

"Accommodating," said Cliff. "What kind of fighter was it?"

"Focke-Schmidt One."

"Focke-Schmidt One?"

"Remember the dope we got out of Lisbon on a new, jet-propelled fighter . . . Messerschmitt wing, the new Serrenbach propulsion unit . . . forty-eight thousand service ceiling and six hundred at thirty thousand?"

"Yes," Garnett nodded, "but Wright Field said it was impossible."

"I know. This is what it does."

Walking over to the board, Dennis stripped back another section of curtain mask, wondering, as he did, how long it had been since Cliff had studied a performance curve. Garnett followed him to the board and ran a swift, expert finger along the co-ordinate lines of the big graph, inked on in different colors, while Dennis watched approvingly.

"These are the tests," said Dennis, indicating rapidly the red, green, yellow, and blue curves. "Thunderbolt, Mustang, Lightning, and Spit 12." Then as he saw Garnett beginning to gape with comprehension he lifted his hand to the heavy black curve so obviously in a class by itself. "And this is the Focke-Schmidt One."

"Jesus Christ!" said Garnett. Then he caught himself and spoke accusingly. "Oh, I see, the German job's in kilometers."

"No it isn't. That's miles, too."

Garnett wheeled from the incontrovertible evidence of the curve.

"Who made these tests?"

"Ted Martin and I."

"You two?"

"Three turns apiece."

67

Garnett traced the black curve with an incredulous finger.

"You did that in your . . . at your age?"

Dennis had prepared himself for this. It was not widely known, even among regulars, that he had been forbidden both speed and oxygen under the bluntest medical warning. His friends were always careful, when something brought it up, to remind him that it was an honorable deficiency. He had burnt out his capacity for extremes in the service. But it still hurt to be less than he had been, to see reservations about himself in other eyes.

In a combat command it had been downright awkward. Kane had advised him to permit issuance of a public statement about why he never flew missions as most generals occasionally did. Dennis knew it was stupid but he had stonily replied that unless his superior believed that it affected the Command's morale adversely he regarded his physical condition as a private matter. Kane had not forced him; he knew, as did the whole service, that in his present condition Dennis could work most men into the ground.

"You shouldn't have done it, Casey," said Garnett.

"I wanted to be sure. It gave me a week in the hospital to think things over afterward."

He was making a mental note to swear Cliff to silence about this when he saw Cathy on his return, but in the midst of it he remembered that he did not yet know whether Cliff was returning. Garnett was tracing the curve again with an awed, rueful finger.

"Well, of course the new Mustang will be a big improvement . . ."

68

"This is not an improvement, Cliff. It's a revolution."

"Yeah. But with enough Mustangs, and the new Thunderbolts . . ."

"Can you arrange an armistice until we get 'em?"

"When will the Germans get these?"

"They've got three factories in line production now. Or rather," he added with a brief smile, "they had day before yesterday. The Czech thinks they already have one group on conversion training. Our Intelligence has lost that group for a month."

"Have you lost any planes to it?"

"Lost planes don't report, Cliff. We've had no sightings from the bombers. But last week we wrote off three reconnaissance planes for the first time in months. They were stripped to the ribs and flying at forty thousand but something got them."

Kane spoke now with a petulance that Dennis understood. He had tried to resist this information himself.

"Of course we don't *know* it was this plane that got them."

"It wasn't mice."

"What about this Czech, Casey? Could this be a double cross?"

Garnett's mind, too, was following the protesting pattern. He was begging for a denial of that curve. Grimly, Dennis went on to explain the other steps of his investigation. He told Garnett how with Kane's permission he had gone down to Whitehall itself, where the gray-faced men worked deep underground behind doors behind doors behind doors. He had a deep respect for Intelligence, the men who dropped into darkness by parachutes, who counterfeited their way into faraway hangars and headquarters. He had come out graver than when he entered.

He told Cliff how Intelligence had traced out the Czech's genealogy, how they had put infra-red cameras on night fighters and photographed the Focke-Schmidts, which only came out of hiding after dark, on the aprons of three camouflaged factory airfields. Then, leaving the graph, Dennis pulled the mask from the operational map and revealed the little triangle of black dots.

"Posenleben, Schweinhafen, and Fendelhorst. That's Operation Stitch, for Stitch in time. . . ."

Garnett whistled. "They're far enough in."

"Marshal Milch thinks better of us these days," said Dennis ruefully.

"What's the present limit of fighter cover, Casey?"

Dennis picked up a piece of blue crayon and swung the arc on the plexiglass map cover. Garnett didn't even bother to reach for the measuring tape. The gap between line and dots was too clear.

As he proceeded with his exposition Dennis noticed that Kane was studying Garnett as intently as Garnett was studying the problem. He had forgotten Cliff's capacity for concentration and for absorbing information rapidly. The counterquestions were pointed and pertinent. Dennis had time to reflect that the United Chiefs probably asked sharp questions, too. He could see that Kane, like himself, was trying to read the Chiefs through their secretary. But it was also part of the secretary's business to keep his thoughts to himself.

Dennis was sure, however, that Garnett comprehended the gravity of this. The struggle for aerial supremacy in Europe was measurable in the multi-colored lines that slashed those quarter-inch crossings of graph paper. It was impossible, of course, to graph so coldly the capabilities of the boys who would work out the proof of this hypothesis. Dennis ran through the last details and came to the climax.

"This curve was made, Cliff, with four 30-millimeter cannon mounted."

He could see Garnett's brief silence reducing this last arithmetic to its shocking significance in range and lethal burst.

"Good God! How were they?"

"Sweet up to thirty-five thousand. That's enough."

It was. Garnett took a long breath.

"Casey, why hasn't this technical data been reported?"

"It has. Through channels. You'll hear from it in about a year."

A rueful nod. Then: —

"What's your honest opinion, Casey?"

"This can run us out of Europe in sixty days."

Kane broke into protest.

"That's giving them absolute perfection in production, in testing, in crew conversion, in armament operation, in spotting, signals, control, tactics . . ." He paused, plainly groping for still further margin between himself and the blunt truth.

"That's giving them thirty days to get two groups operational and thirty more to catch one of our columns for just half an hour, sir. I put that in the report, Cliff."

"Why didn't you send this report to us?" asked Garnett.

Dennis did not answer. Garnett turned from him slowly for a deliberate, inquiring scrutiny of Kane. The Major General stirred like a man trying to shake off a bad dream.

"I couldn't endorse such alarming conclusions, Cliff. This would disturb the United Chiefs at the very time when everything depends on our getting well established here, on an acceptable loss basis, for the good of the whole service."

"You didn't agree with the report then, sir?"

"Nobody could prove these assumptions now," said Kane angrily. "We have experimental jobs of our own that could be hotted up to test like that with Ted or Casey flying. I did send a preliminary appreciation that we could not exclude the possibility of encountering an unsuspected enemy capability."

"Did you approve this Operation Stitch, sir?"

Kane's ruddy face was dark purple.

"I told General Dennis that this operation constitutes a tactical emergency within the scope of division commanders' directives. If, in his opinion, the threat justifies countermeasures . . ."

"That's my opinion, Cliff," said Dennis. "It's my rap."

Kane flashed him a grateful glance but Garnett shook his head.

"Your losses are the United Chiefs' rap, Casey. As a matter of fact that's what I'm over here about. A lot of our people were very upset, even before yesterday. A very substantial body of opinion still doesn't believe we can succeed with daylight precision bombardment."

"A very substantial body of opinion didn't believe in the Wright brothers, either."

"It isn't quite that simple, Casey. This program is making a terrible drain on our overall resources of the very best manpower and matériel. I may as well tell you that the United Chiefs are having another Global Allocation meeting on Tuesday."

There was instant relief in realizing what had been wrong with Kane today. He had already known this, Dennis gathered.

"Tuesday . . . I've had to wait three weeks for this run of weather, Cliff. You can only count on about one three-day run a summer here. But we got Posenleben yesterday and Schweinhafen today and this is only Saturday. Weather thinks it will be okay for Fendelhorst tomorrow. We can finish before that meeting can do anything to us."

"Have you thought what losses like this might do to that meeting?"

He had been thinking of exactly that. Kane took up the slack of the silence.

"This could upset the whole larger picture, Casey."

"Would you rather have Goering upset it, sir?"

"That's *still* an assumption," said Kane plaintively. "The overall plan calls for me . . . for us to have the largest bomber force in the Hemisphere. These two days are going to be a terrible shock to the Chiefs, Casey. I'm not at all sure that, for the good of the whole service, I'm justified in permitting a third . . ."

"You've got to, sir," snapped Dennis. "Concentration is the crux of this matter. You agreed to that before I started."

"Why? Why just now?" inquired Garnett.

"Weather," said Dennis. "It may be a month before we can get back to Fendelhorst. These two attacks have tipped our hand. Half the rolling flak in Germany is probably on its way there right now. They'll either make it impregnable or disperse that machinery until we never find it unless we get it in the next forty-eight hours."

Garnett nodded absently but his frown reflected a detachment from such details as European weather. Kane and Dennis regarded each other stonily. Then, even before their ears could hear the first faint roaring, the three men with one accord made for the windows as everything else in their minds gave way to the pressure of the returning Fortresses.

Chapter Four

THEY CAME FAST and, this afternoon, low. The first seemed to spring out of the treetops across the field. The sight of them steadied Dennis.

Two others darting in from another angle were already above him now, bulky and ugly as they always appeared at these deceptive short angles. Both were yawing jerkily from the grasping suction of gaping shot holes. But they had zigzagged that way from Germany and their motors were steady. They would make it to the ground. He dismissed them, extending his quick estimates to the next ones with the hot familiar pain kneading his stomach as he did.

They were badly scattered. He knew that they usually broke formation about mid-Channel after a run like this one but more than drying gas tanks had spread them out today. As his eyes assessed the damage expertly he realized that he had not yet seen two of them which could have flown closely enough to each other to make normal formation safe . . . five . . . six . . . eight . . . he did not know that he was counting aloud unconsciously as every pair of lips on the station always counted. He could hear Garnett's low exclamation distinctly.

"Look at those props!"

He had counted six feathered ones himself before the building shook with the wash of the planes immediately overhead and the Forts vanished, leaving the sky behind them still athrob with their receding vibrations. Dennis wet his lips and knew with minor comfort that he was not going to puke today, bad as it was.

"I made it eleven."

"So did I," said Garnett. "What's squadron strength?"

"Twelve, if it was a squadron."

Kane blenched visibly. "That isn't the remains of a Group, is it, Casey?"

"I can't tell yet, sir."

Kane exploded: "Well, find out! Find out at once."

Dennis had to check himself. Kane was not as used to this as he was. Without risking a reply he strode rapidly through the Ops room door and closed it behind him. The room quieted; the vibration of this particular bunch was lost now in the gentle sea of lesser vibrations coming from every side as the remainder of the Division converged around the other near-by bases.

With the departure of Dennis, Kane took a conscious grip on himself and turned from the window to Garnett, who was still staring out speechless at what he had seen.

"Cliff, what will Washington think of this?"

It took Cliff several seconds to clear that spectacle from his mind. When he had done it he measured his words gravely.

"I wish they'd had some preparation, sir."

"I never dreamed Casey would be so . . . so impetuous."

"Can you reach Washington by telephone, sir?"

"Not from here. I can by teleprinter conversation from Joe Endicott's division, forty miles from here. Cliff, you don't think a . . . a misfortune now could really affect overall allocation, do you?"

Garnett thought aloud: "Two successive loss records . . . 20 to 25 per cent . . . with no warning . . ."

"We'll have claims though . . . records claims. The Chief loves those."

"I'm not thinking of our Chief, sir."

He was spared further consideration for the moment by Prescott, who hurried in, and by Brockhurst, who sauntered slowly after.

"Sir, Brockie has some ideas I think you should hear."

"All right, Brockie. Tell us frankly."

Brockhurst studied Kane's evident agitation and let him wait a little. He still resented his eviction from the military council. He had kept the secrets of bigger men than Kane and he was always infuriated by the army's assumption that no one out of uniform was trustworthy.

From Prescott he had learned all he needed to know about the Jenks case; but he was after bigger game. He needed Kane's help and he wanted Kane to understand that he was going to help.

"You want it rough or smooth, R. G.?" he asked quietly.

"Let's have it."

"Your neck's out a foot."

"*My* neck . . . ?"

"It's your baby unless you can buck it up to the Hemisphere Commander. You've got a hero to court-martial and you've got losses that'll sound like Verdun in America. You've let this Secret Security Policy of yours keep the whole deal so dark it's going to look like

77

a cover for the worst blunder since Pearl Harbor. After all, the public makes these bombers and sends you these kids, it's got a right to know . . ."

He stopped as Dennis hurried in from the Ops room still smoldering with suppressed anger. The very force of it made even Kane glance at him apprehensively; his voice was oddly conciliatory.

"Casey, Elmer here is giving us his reaction. I want you to hear it."

"He knows it," said Brockhurst. "I tried to warn him that the press and public . . ."

"Press and public be goddamned," said Dennis. "Your syndicate would ambush a whole division for one head-line and then print enough crocodile tears to keep us from ever making a useful attack again."

"When did we ever . . . ?"

"After Bremfurt. We needed a second attack to finish that job. By the time you got done with our losses and Washington got done explaining your in-sinuations, we got an order that it was politically im-possible to attack the place again. *Politically impossible!* Some of our boys were killed today with cannon made at Bremfurt since that attack."

Brockhurst subsided. It was useless to explain now that he himself had been heartily ashamed of what his people had made of that unfortunate episode. Kane turned aside the Brigadier's wrath.

"Was that a group or a squadron, General?"

"The 641st Group, sir. Some stragglers are still com-ing."

"How many?"

"Three reported so far, sir."

78

They were all thinking the same thing. Kane said it.

"Fourteen out of thirty-six."

"Thirty-four, sir; two aborted this morning."

Kane shuddered. "That's over 50 per cent."

"Nearly 59, sir," said Major Prescott.

"How about the other groups, General?"

"Incomplete, so far, sir. Radio silence is still on except for serious cripples."

They regarded each other through a short, heavy silence. The vibrations of the homing Forts were almost imperceptible. Kane cleared his throat.

"See if you can get anything more, will you, General?"

Dennis understood that this second dismissal from his own office was less a rebuke than a precaution. He was now ashamed of having lost his temper at that miserable reporter. He knew that his self-control was always overtaxed while Ted was out. He welcomed the excuse to hurry into the Ops room where he could be that much nearer the teleprinter. Kane waited to speak until the door was closed behind Dennis.

"Of course the other groups may not be so bad."

"They better not be," said Brockhurst.

"I'm afraid you're right. I warned General Dennis . . ."

"Dennis hell! Do you think a brigadier's a big enough burnt offering for a fiasco like this?"

Brockhurst could see Garnett stiffen with disapproval at this but he didn't care.

"It's not a fiasco, Brockie. If the public realized . . ."

"I'm the public and I don't realize a damned thing. Anything you say afterwards is just alibis, R. G."

"We'll have claims, record claims."

"All smoke clouds look alike. When there isn't any story . . ."

Kane strode angrily to the wall and stripped back the curtain mask from the operational map. Garnett almost spoke in protest and then with a visible effort checked himself.

"Story!" said Kane furiously. "Story? It's the most audacious air operation in history. Two successive strikes at the most distant and dangerous targets ever attacked in daylight . . . the very guts and core of Germany's new fighter program. Look at this!"

He jabbed a savage finger into the red cross over Posenleben and then, seizing a red crayon from the tray, made a heavy red cross through Schweinhafen.

"Hold it," said Brockhurst. "I want a shot of that."

"We'll get you a clean map, Brockie," said Major Prescott.

"No. I want Kane himself, crossing it off . . ."

His own interest had betrayed him. Covering his enthusiasm now he concluded slowly: ". . . that is, if I do the story."

"Now listen, Brockie . . ."

"Or maybe there's another story, an inside story that I don't see. But I'd have to see it all, exclusively."

They all turned to see that Dennis had paused in the doorway, his eyes hard at the sight of the correspondent peering at the uncovered operational map. This time, however, he had his temper firmly in control.

"Preliminary count thirty-five missing with one group unreported as yet, sir."

"About 32 per cent, sir," said Major Prescott. And

at that moment they were silenced by the rising vibrations of the last group of returning Fortresses.

2

Evans, waiting on call in the General's anteroom, had decided it was about time to break up the meeting. Ordinarily he was delighted to doze at leisure through the brayings of the brass but today other considerations were stirring him. He needed freedom of action to remove the musette bag full of whiskey from the non-secret filing cases in the crowded cubicle where he sat. Yet beyond even this consideration Evans found himself pondering whether the termination of the conference would be good for General Dennis. The discovery that he was concerned about the General's welfare disturbed him.

For the dozenth time he reassured himself indignantly that he didn't give a damn what became of Dennis or any other general. If he didn't like this Garnett he would move on. He had long since learned that, with reason, a resourceful man could do whatever he liked in the army.

Regulars made a fetish of doing things they did not like in the name of duty, but Regulars liked being in the army and enjoyed kicking each other around. Evans felt that that was their business. Anyone who wanted to spend twenty or twenty-five years waiting for automatic promotions to change the ratio between the men he could boss and the men who could boss him was welcome to it.

In civil life Evans had been a lineman. He had enjoyed beating the draft systematically until the morning after Pearl Harbor. That day the company superintendent had come out to the pole yard and told the men they were not to worry. Line work was a vital facet of national defense and the company would take care of all of them. That afternoon Evans enlisted.

He had known that his occupational experience would lead him straight to the Signal Corps. He knew also that telephones were made for talking. Talking was not going to end this war and Evans had no intention of climbing poles for the government for sixty dollars a month. In the induction center he signed himself down as a clerk.

In the next six months three lieutenants, two captains, and one major had eagerly approved his requests for transfer. The major had debated between approving his request to go to gunnery school and trying him for the willful mishandling of government records. But the unit had to make up a quota of volunteer gunners. He had made an excellent gunner and, during his tour, an exemplary soldier. He knew that on at least two occasions he personally had saved the government three hundred thousand dollars' worth of airplane, once over Münster and once over the Channel.

The lives of his fellow crew members did not enter this calculation because most of them had done as much for him at one time or another, which made it a private and human matter beyond the government's province. He did feel, however, that two planes was a fair exchange for even his impressive ribbons. Many men had filed higher claims than his but Evans had observed that the ones who did were usually sent posthaste back to the States for teaching after their tours. He wanted no part of teaching. He considered that he and the government were now at honorable quits; they wouldn't let him out of service of course but neither would they make him climb poles for sixty bucks a month, if he kept his neck in.

Until today his post-tour life had been complicated by no deeper purpose than enjoying his leisure and keeping the Regulars in their place. Now against all reason and experience he found himself pondering whether or not it would help General Dennis to have him break up the jawing in the office.

Crossing the anteroom toward the door, Evans too began to feel the rising roar of the last returning group. One of them, his experienced ears told him, was having a hell of a time. He stopped in his tracks, measuring the continuous increase and its internal communications carefully. The man had no more than two motors and was coming straight for them but he probably had altitude enough to clear the building. Evans hoped he had been able to get rid of his bombs.

Inside the office Evans found all three Generals, the Major, and the correspondent grouped tensely as they peered out of the window. The noise of the oncoming planes made it useless to speak. Evans took up his position by the door.

Dennis, even through the tension of his careful, habitual counting, had switched his eyes from their first glimpse of the crippled ship to the crash crews and ambulances waiting by the Ops tower. Everything was all right. The asbestos suits were buckled and steady streams of exhaust were pluming out of both vehicles. He saw that Major Dayhuff and Captain Getchell were both getting into the ambulance in white surgical coats and he made a mental note to speak to them that evening himself. He appreciated the instincts that made them both go rather than send their lieutenants but it was not their job.

Across the field he saw the long line of the Group's noncombat personnel lined up against the barrier ropes, the long dark blur of their fatigues broken here and there by the white of cooks and mess helpers. Every man among them, he knew, was watching and counting as tensely as he was.

" . . . eighteen . . . twenty . . . twenty-one . . ." it looked a little better this time except for that one bad cripple and the fact that he still had not seen the un-corseted girl on the nose of the plane Ted was riding . . . "twenty-three . . ."

"God, that one's low!" said Garnett behind him.

It was the cripple and even as he was trying to see whether the man had any undercarriage he could clearly hear Prescott's fatuous remark.

"When a crew finishes a tour, sir, they always give the field a good buzz in spite of rules."

The plane zoomed down at them, so low now that even the men across the field threw themselves on the ground. In the room, its sound had become a continuous thunder. Through it Dennis could hear the shouts of the men behind him and then the thudding of their bodies on the floor but he was scarcely aware of them. He was trying to measure the boy's chances. As the plane cleared them with a crescendo of thunder perhaps two hundred feet above the building, Dennis saw that he had one sound motor and heard a second one catch with a rough, protesting response to the momentum of the zoom. It was skipping but as the noise receded Dennis could tell that the boy had recaptured some of the pull in it.

Turning back now from the momentarily blank sky he observed that Kane, Garnett, Brockhurst, and Prescott were still trying to get their noses into the floorboards, their elbows drawn tightly over their ears. Beyond them Evans was regarding the spectacle with a sardonic smile that vanished slowly from his face as they began to peer up into the relative quiet of the plane's receding thunder.

"Colonel Martin's group returning, sir," said Evans dryly.

Kane gathered himself first and jumped up. The others followed sheepishly, the more chagrined to realize that neither Dennis nor Evans had left his feet.

"I'll have that man tried," said Kane. "After my orders about buzzing . . ."

Dennis, his face glued to the window, had to speak over his shoulder.

"He isn't buzzing, sir. He's in trouble."

They had gathered again behind him and he could hear their dismay as the plane came back into sight on a wide, approaching circle.

"My God!" whispered Garnett. "Two feathered and one windmilling."

"Half the tail's gone," said Prescott.

"How in God's name is he turning it?" breathed Kane.

Dennis himself didn't know. He was flying it in with his own tendons now. He could feel them flexing and giving with the yawing erratic course of the ship, even though his mind knew that the boy up there probably didn't have a quarter of his controls left. Incredibly, though, he had not only turned but was actually managing to lift it a little as the increase in the vibrations began to hammer them again.

"Why don't they bail out? She's only salvage."

He felt a sudden fury that Garnett, of all people, should presume to question anything that boy was doing.

"Probably wounded aboard," he grunted.

As if in confirmation they suddenly saw the red rockets flowering out behind her and then, from the left waistgate, three black balls appeared against the blueness of the sky.

"Look! They are bailing . . . two, three . . . look, they're opening all right. Jesus! They didn't have three hundred feet!" shouted Garnett.

Dennis had felt with his whole body the lifting of the ship as those jumping figures lightened it. Now his tendons were taut again with the climbing curve that boy still, against all possibility, maintained. To the last possible second of the feud between gravity and momentum the boy held that bank. Then, as gravity won and the ship had to sag heavily back to level or spin in, he saw her settling in a smooth straight glide and realized that the pilot had succeeded in lining her up for the Number Two Strip with geometrical precision.

"Good boy," he breathed, "he's going to try it."

She was so close now that they could plainly see her

markings. As her last motor throttled down a little for the final shaky glide, the growling of the gear in the ambulance beside the Ops tower broke through the slackening volume of sound.

"*Urgent Virgin!*" said Garnett.

"Why, that's Captain Jenks's ship!" exclaimed Prescott.

Her struggle was almost over now. Gravity was claiming her with harsh jerks that slewed her savagely from side to side against the failing resistance of momentum and the clutching suction of the cannon wounds. It was one of these helpless, sidewise flutterings that suddenly showed Dennis the condition of her right wheel. He shouted.

"Pick her up, boy! PICK HER UP!"

He knew it was hopeless and knew that the boy himself must know it. He should be getting them away from the glass of the window but he stood immovable, watching. The *Urgent Virgin* seemed to settle very slowly now. With a final birdlike gentleness she leveled off perfectly just as the broken wheel strut touched down. Game to the last, she even bounced a little as the strut sheered off, but the lame motor would not respond this time and the last one could not do it. As if in slow motion she teetered a little twice more at the crest of her bounce and then, at a long final angle, plowed herself in. The ripping, tearing noises faded slowly into silence and then the detonation fluttered the maps tacked on the wall. Fragments appeared, arching lazily upward out of the expanding cloud of dust and smoke.

Dennis made himself listen intently a second more but he could hear no screaming through the brief interval before the roaring motors of the crash truck and ambulance punctured the silence. He turned from the window, shoulders sagging limply, to find himself looking into the green fixity of Major Prescott's face.

"There's another statistic for you, Major," he said harshly.

Haley appeared in the Ops room door.

"Left main gas tank. Category E, sir."

"Can you get the others down here?"

"We're taking cripples on Strip One and sending everything with enough gas to the 641st. There's lots of room over there now, sir."

"Any count on this gang yet?"

"Twenty-eight now, sir. There may be stragglers."

He held Haley with his eyes, knowing it was no oversight which kept the Colonel silent now. Haley would have spoken at once if he had anything more to say. But Dennis could not help asking him.

"Anything on Ted himself?"

"Not yet, sir."

"Get an aggregate for tomorrow's serviceability from all groups as fast as possible."

Haley vanished. Dennis faced Kane steadily.

"Looks like forty-two, sir, with two in the ditch."

"Worse than yesterday," said Kane softly.

"They got their target, sir."

Evans decided this had gone far enough. Stepping forward he addressed himself with a bland face to General Kane.

"Does the General want the photographers in here or outside, sir?"

Kane looked as nonplused as Evans had known he would. It was Prescott who saw his superior's indecision and turned severely on Evans.

"What photographers, Sergeant?"

"From Division, Wing and Groups Publicity, sir."

"Who ordered them and on what authority?"

"I did, sir. All generals have their pictures taken wherever they go. They say it helps the boys' morale, sir."

Prescott was still wondering how to deal with this straight-faced insolence when the General smiled appreciatively on Evans.

"Well, of course if it helps morale . . ." He picked up his cap, straightened his blouse a little, and extended the smile to Dennis. "We'll be going along, General . . . probably drop in on some of your interrogations at the groups."

Dennis picked up his own cap. "As you say, sir."

"No, no, my boy. I wouldn't think of taking you away from here just now. Get me that claims total as soon as possible and be sure to get good pictures of the battle damage today."

"As you say, sir."

Kane ushered the rest of them ahead of him now rapidly, and as they paused at the door to let him go out first he spoke hastily over his shoulder.

"Don't send tomorrow's field order until I get back."

"Very well, sir."

As the anteroom door closed on them Dennis whirled and put his head into the Ops room. Haley had his eyes riveted on the teleprinter and headphones on his ears but instinct brought him to rigid attention even before Dennis barked at him.

"Anything on Ted yet?"

"Not yet, sir."

He slammed the door and began walking a tight tense circle around the office, consciously keeping away from the window with its view of the burning *Virgin*. He couldn't help that now; he couldn't help any of it. He had to get himself together against the night's work. The return of Evans helped. He stopped in his tracks and regarded the Sergeant quizzically. He was going to speak to him about his manners one day. But some deep, warming instinct told Dennis that Evans's manners this afternoon had been intentional.

"One of these days you're going to wisecrack yourself right into the infantry, Sergeant."

"Sir, if I hadn't told 'em they was cameras outside we never would have got rid of them."

The candor of the confession was completely disarming. This was plain, sly insubordination. Rebuking it would be ingratitude. Dennis tried to sound severely impersonal.

"They're coming back. Alert the cook and get the guest hut ready just in case."

"Sir, maybe if I was to speak to the cook . . ."

"None of that. We'll have to give them a good dinner."

As Evans went out Dennis reflected that if the boy hadn't been a combat gunner he really would have spoken to him. He heard the footsteps recede through the anteroom and then, apparently, turn back with a lighter, quicker approaching beat. He set his face and made up his mind that if Evans should be up to further deviltry, he would speak to him this time for his own good. Then, with the opening of the door, he felt himself go a little limp and sat down quickly in the chair by the map table as Ted Martin walked in, grinning.

Chapter Five

DENNIS HAD been through this often enough to recover rapidly. The first confirmation of Ted's safety seemed always to paralyze him.

It was so now. Ted's normal buoyancy was sagging. The deep grime on his face was powder smoke, slashed with an inverted V that outlined the sides of his nose with a telltale imprint of skin washed clean by sweat and tears along the edges of his oxygen mask. Then, for the first time, Dennis saw the large dark blotches of dried blood on the white silk scarf and dirty coveralls. Yet Ted had walked in lightly, grinning.

"You all right?"

"Not a scratch."

"What's that blood?"

The grin faded. "My radioman."

"Bad?"

"Dead."

He saw now that the blood patches extended even to Ted's hands. He must have taken off his gloves but his fingers showed none of the puffy discoloration of freezing.

"Anyone else?"

"Not in our plane. Got a drink?"

Dennis was in self-possession again as he fetched the bottle from his desk and extended it to Ted.

"Aren't they serving combat ration?"

"Yeah, but I wanted to see you quick. Hell, Casey,

92

this is your last and I've drunk nearly half of it already."

"That's what it's for."

Ted drank from the bottle with long greedy gulps but Dennis knew that he could empty it, and probably would, without showing the effect. The fierce inner combustion that produced his unique vitality seemed to absorb alcohol for fuel. Dennis noticed that he was bloodstained all the way down to his socks but the face that reappeared from behind the bottle was grinning again now.

"What happened?"

"Twenty millimeter right on the radio panel." Ted poured some more whiskey right through his uptilted throat. "Mmmm, that's better. I always said we should have fought this war ten years ago."

"How do you think I feel?"

Ted covered his instant contrition with impudence. "Sorry, Grandpa," said he and drank again.

Dennis regretted the inadvertence. He didn't begrudge Ted's five years of advantage and it was useless to harp on it. At that moment Haley walked in on them, his instant grin at the sight of Ted disappearing into a sober formality.

"Another straggler from the 693rd, sir. Landed away from base."

"In a village, I suppose?"

"No, sir." Haley permitted himself another smile. "Open field and no one injured. Category E, though."

"Good." The whole day was improving. With his duty done Haley now considered it permissible to express a personal feeling.

"I'm glad you got back today, Ted."

93

"So am I." Martin grinned and thrust the bottle forward. "Shot, Ernie?"

"*Now* . . .?" Haley always took one Scotch and soda in the Officers' Club bar before dinner on nights when the board was scrubbed, if there was Scotch. . . . "Thanks, Ted. Maybe I'll have one with you before dinner."

He hurried out, a little embarrassed by Martin's open laughter but eager to tell the Adjutant that Ted was back. He decided in fact to tell the whole office. It would cheer everyone up.

"Tell me about it," said Dennis. "Rough all the way?"

Ted wiped his mouth on a bloody sleeve, stuck a cigarette into his face, sat down, and lifted his flying boots comfortably up onto the map table, nursing the bottle in his lap.

"No. Milk run for thirty-four minutes after our fighters turned back. Then the whole damned G.A.F. jumped us." He laughed suddenly. "Those guys must have a new directive over there, too. From then back to our fighters was almost continuous. Our fighters were swell today, too, Casey. From the way they hung on I bet some of 'em had to get out and push the last mile home."

"When did you get yours?"

"Just after the strike flash. What about the rest?"

"Looks like forty-one now, with two in the ditch."

"I was afraid of that from what I saw."

"Did you catch fire?"

"Yeah. We were having it hot and heavy so I stayed on the nose gun and Goldberg went back and put it out.

He should get something for it, too. One of our waist gunners took one look at that fire and went right out through the bomb bay. I bet he's playing checkers with their Intelligence right now."

Dennis considered the various pieces of ribbon and metal which they might give Goldberg for having successfully plied a fire extinguisher between two tankfuls of high-octane gasoline four and a half miles above Germany in a hail of incendiary bullets and explosive flak.

"Goldberg can have what you recommend," he said.

"I'll think it over. Then, after things quieted down, we tried a tourniquet on the kid but it was too late."

Martin shook his head, drank hard, and then put the bottle on the table with an air of coming to business.

"Didn't I just see Percent and Cliff Garnett in a car?"

"Yeah," said Dennis. "The joint's full of big wheels today."

"Did Cliff bring any news of Helen?"

"Letters; there's no cable. I've been checking."

"Thanks. Casey, what's Cliff doing so far from home?"

"Visiting, he says."

"How long?"

"Well," Dennis hesitated, "he intimated just routine rubbernecking and high-level courier stuff."

"Intimated?"

It was always useless to pretend with Ted. But before he had to say anything further Evans appeared in the anteroom door.

"Sir, what do you want done with General Garnett's foot locker and bedroll?"

Ted repeated after him, "Garnett's foot locker and bedroll?"

"They just came in, sir. Glad you're back, Colonel Martin."

"Put them in the Number One guest hut," said Dennis.

As Evans closed the door Martin jumped up and faced Dennis, his habitual grin a little awry. "Turn around, Casey."

Dennis did and felt fingers massaging his shoulder blades. He began to grin himself even before Martin spoke.

"Well, the handle doesn't stick out, anyway."

"Colonel," said Dennis dryly, "you are speaking of your revered brother-in-law and a General Officer in the United States Army."

Martin did not respond; his voice had become serious.

"Any brigadier in the army would give his next star for your job, Casey."

Dennis knew it was true. Incredible and remote as it all seemed now, he himself had dreamed of this job before getting it.

"When I finish Stitch they can have it for corporal's stripes. Thank God we're two-thirds done."

Martin looked at the bottle. Then, turning away from it, he shook his head slowly at Dennis.

"Casey, that's the hell of it. We aren't."

"Aren't what! You did Poseleben yesterday and Schweinhafen today. . . ."

"We didn't touch Schweinhafen today. . . ." Dennis could see that Ted was sober and struggling to force the words out. "We plastered some goddamned place that looked exactly like it, forty miles from Schweinhafen."

96

2

Dennis arose from his seat, took a long look at the whiskey bottle. Then he circled the room slowly twice, stopping for a long look at the sky through the window before he broke the silence.

"How did it happen?"

"Sighting mistake," said Martin. "It was my fault, Casey. When we came to the I. P. there was a little cloud and we were fighting hard. I got one quick gander and it looked like Bindlegarsten so I turned the column. When we came on our run there sat a little town that looked more like Schweinhafen than Schweinhafen does; same confluence of rivers, railroad, and highway, same cathedral a mile to the left, same airfield, same phoney road on the roof camouflage. I was still on the nose gun but I switched with Jake long enough for a look through the sight myself. We were both sure of it and Jake threw the whole load right down the chimney. The others salvoed into our smoke."

"How do you know it wasn't Schweinhafen?" Dennis knew that he was simply resisting this as Garnett's mind had resisted that performance graph. It was equally useless and he could see that it was hurting Ted to tell him, but he needed time to face the whole thing.

"Because when we got our fire out and I got time to look down again there was Nurenover and we'd been rallying north."

"Sure you weren't turned around in the fighting?"

"I swung east, even with the fighting, to make sure.

There was Schweinhafen without a scratch. I'm sorry, Casey."

"Why didn't you correct your strike signal?"

"My radioman was dead and the radio was blown all over Bavaria. I'd sent the flash before I realized the mistake."

Haley stuck his head into the doorway. "Embassy in London calling General Kane, sir."

"He's visiting groups. Pick him up on a multiple. And put a red-line security stop to all groups on any mention of today's target; same for the theater censor."

Ted nodded approval but he waited for Haley to close the door before speaking. "Did you tell Kane we'd hit it?"

"Yes."

"Has he announced it?"

"Not yet. This will stop it. What do you think you did hit?"

"Goldberg's checking maps and photos and target folders now," said Ted, shrugging. "Whatever it was came apart like a powder mill."

They looked at each other through a short silence. Haley stuck his head through the door again.

"Stop's on, sir. And we've found another straggler. That leaves forty unreported and two in the ditch, so far."

"Battle damage?"

"They're still estimating, sir. Looks rough."

As Haley vanished this time Martin shook his head slowly.

"Why don't you castrate me?"

"You've had this coming. It's averages, Ted."

"Maybe. But what's it going to do to Stitch?"

98

Dennis forced a smile which he hoped looked natural.

"Set us back a day. We'll do Schweinhafen tomorrow and Fendelhorst Monday. I think the weather will hold."

"Will Kane?"

"He'll have to."

"Casey, he had cold feet before we started. I doubt if he ever came clean with Washington. What do you think he's going to say to this?"

Dennis shrugged. "Just another casualty for Operation Stitch."

"Casey!" Martin had come alive again now with hot, concerned protest. "Quit hurting about casualties. Most of these guys would be killed in a normal tour anyway. We've been through that before. This way they're doing something that counts instead of running up phony statistics for that old . . ."

"Ted, he's our chief."

"Sure! Sure he's our chief. And a good soldier is loyal. It says so in the book. But what's he loyal to, anyway . . . to mortal, fallible men above him, half the time dopes and cowards with shelves full of rules they've made to protect themselves . . . or is he loyal to his own common sense . . . and to guys who have to do things that aren't in the books, like Stitch? You better get your head out of the clouds before you lose it, Casey."

It was an old argument between them.

"Kane didn't forbid Stitch, Ted."

"Did he authorize it? Did he attend his weather conferences and go on record like a man? Not Kane. You're the goat on this one."

"Other guys have been killed. If I get canned . . ."

"If you get canned it's the end of honest bombard-

99

ment here and you know it! We'll piddle away our planes building statistics over France while they build a defense over Germany that will make today's losses look like a sprained ankle."

Even through the Ops room door Haley could hear the crackling fury of Martin's voice and it made him shudder. He knew that the men had been inseparable friends for fifteen years but he considered that only the more reason why Martin should have been more discreet. It was true that Martin always behaved with correct subordination when the two were in public but now half the building could hear his anger, if not his words. Most major generals would not have used that tone on Dennis. Some of the enlisted men were openly smiling now and Haley was glad of an excuse to enter the room. He found the two deadlocked, but as always they shut up in the presence of anyone else.

"The Hemisphere Commander's Public Relations Officer is calling General Kane, sir."

"I told you he's at a group, probably in an Interrogation hut. And let me speak to him before any P.R.O. does."

This time Martin's heedless vehemence did not even await the full closing of the door.

"You *can't* tell him, Casey. You're protecting him not to. And what about the guys we've already lost? If Kane quits now they're wasted. We've either got to finish now or we might as well take this Air Army back to Arizona. It's us or them, this week, boy, and you're the only guy in the hemisphere with guts enough to see it through."

"How . . . if we don't tell him?" asked Dennis warily.

"Let him be happy with today's pictures. Tomorrow we'll knock off Fendelhorst. Then Monday, when he orders his usual month-end milk run to Calais or Dunkirk we'll go back and clean up Schweinhafen."

It was so exactly what Dennis had been thinking himself that he could not suppress a guilty start. Of course it was natural; his mind and Ted's had been working together for fifteen years. Even now Ted was watching him measuring it, following his clear understanding that it was a workable expedient. The return of Haley gave him a minute more.

"Sixty-sixth Wing reports both of today's reconnaissance planes now four hours overdue, sir."

Dennis cleared his head with a hard shake. "Keep that battle damage coming. I'll call General Kane myself, Haley."

This time as Haley closed the door Martin jumped up, placing himself between Dennis and the phones on the desk.

"Casey, today it's recce planes; six weeks from now it will be whole divisions unless we finish this job."

"We'll finish, Ted. We'll make him finish."

He confronted Martin a second more, his face muscles struggling with his effort to make them show more assurance than he felt. He knew that he should take more time to think this through but he did not dare. He stepped past Martin decisively now; he had to do it and he had to do it fast, before he did think any more. Martin's face was aghast under its powder smoke as he picked up the phone.

"You're going to tell him?"

"He's the Chief."

101

Chapter Six

LONG BEFORE the late nightfall of the British summer the Division Headquarters and its outlying stations again took on the accelerating pulsations of activity.

There was a rhythmic cycle in this life that began its slow rise once more from the final counting in after the mission. For the combat crews this was an ending; another mission checked off, another restorative interlude for the brief unreality of food and sleep, of music, games, or women. Especially after a second successive long mission pure fatigue claimed most of them.

Only a hardy few, those whose natural energy was inexhaustible, those whose nervous structures could not unwind, those who had taken benzedrine too late, lingered on at the mess, thumbed through the records in the lounge, changing them after the first few bars of each tune, and then sat looking numbly at the barren expanse of the V-mail blanks or, taking their bicycles from the racks, wheeled out of the station in quest of different excitement.

Most of the men, with a headshake at that serene twilight sky, made straight for the sack, there to snore or lie tense, trying to evoke the smell of hamburger in juke joints or the patterns of moonlight on country club terraces as the fragments of the phonograph tunes echoed on the corrugated iron roofs.

In the villages around them girls who had learned the

102

new portents of peaceful heavens saw the hope vanishing and settled again to another twenty-four hours of dread. And through their ears, as through those of farmers and villagers, of crews tossing in their cots, of hares and partridge chicks and foxes prowling the beetroot and kale patches in the Lincolnshire gloaming, there drummed now from every side in universal chorus the rising hum of myriad motors tuning.

For now the work of the base personnel rose with a jerky tempo to the tune of the motors. Along the lanes muffled jeep lights bounced crazily over bumps their dim projection had not revealed. Down by the bomb dumps panting tractors chugged the dollies into place. Then their crews cut their switches and paced off through the cool grass the requisite distance for smoking while they watched the coming of the evening stars and waited the details of the loading decision.

Along every highway, through every station, around every perimeter track, and to every parking stand the petrol trucks rumbled on the last lap of the journey that had brought their cargo through sub-haunted waters from Arabia and the Caribbean. Deft hands and wrenches maneuvered the hoses. Then with the soft whirring of still more motors the weary truck tires began to contract again and the bulbous doughnuts of the Fortresses spread and distended under the inflowing burden as dry tanks gurgled and burped.

Now above and around the Forts themselves, on platforms and catwalks and cowlings, with chain hoists that lifted motors like matches and wrenches smaller than matches, the crews clambered and cursed and toiled in a disciplined frenzy of activity. Motors coughed and spluttered, roared into thunder or choked into vacuums of quick silence. Starting engines whined and squealed, generators purred. Hammers and scissors, files and hacksaws and riveters, incised with sure surgery around the gaping shot wounds, ripping, replacing, restoring, and finally polishing new strength and surface into the old contours of the bodies. In the motors themselves men stripped and dismantled and searched, deeper and ever deeper seeking with calipers and gauges and electric pulsations the subtler maladies of friction and metal fatigue.

In the gloom muffled work lamps twinkled like fireflies. Wrenches slipped, skin vanished into long bleeding cuts. Lungs coughed with protest against ubiquitous monoxide. Voices rose with cursing or exultation. Hurrying chiefs looked oftener and oftener at their watches. Every passing bicycle or jeep slowed up to receive or pass on with blasphemy the information that there was as yet no further information.

In the cook shacks other men waited for the word. Already the standard things were done. Bread was baking, beans boiling, stew meat and potatoes poured from the machines into rising conicles in the great caldrons. Cans gasped under the knives and then yielded their contents with a gurgle. But there too the absence of final word delayed the final arrangements. The padlocks guarding the combat crews' fresh eggs and oranges were still locked. Their keys remained deep in the pockets of scowling mess sergeants who pondered the comic strips in the *Stars and Stripes* spread out on their tables as they, too, waited.

Outside the staff offices at both Division and Group Headquarters the continuous opening and shutting of doors slashed the blackout with quick shards of the bright internal light, as men hurried to and fro, exchanging with each other the news that there was no news yet.

They too were cursing the delay. The chairs were set and the blackboard sponged against the morning's briefing. But the tiered cords of maps waited in their bins until it was decided which particular acres of them must be folded and marked long before take-off. In other rooms men fingered and studied blankly the miniature planes whose numbers duplicated those on the monsters now gutted for repair work on the parking stands. Each phone call was a resurrection, moving one of the symbols into its place in the toy formation on the blackboard which would precede and dictate tomorrow's formation in the sky . . . if there was to be a formation.

Through all of these and a hundred other forms of preparation men worked always with uncertainty in their minds, measuring everything they did by it. Every part of the process could be brought so far, and nightly was brought so far, toward the final forms of preparation. This in itself was more than enough to occupy most of the men most of the night. But in itself this also was only a preliminary to the final frenzy which would begin with the certainty of a mission and then the unfolding final details of bomb load, gas load, degrees of repair, destination, courses, timings, frequencies, and all the other innumerable and vital details which must somehow be worked out through the steadily dwindling interval to the deadline of the take-off.

2

Dennis knew very well not only the continuously changing physical condition of his command throughout this vigil but its emotional and nervous state. It had been his life's work to control and manage the energies of other men, training and restraining them until orders gave them final release in purpose for which there never could be entirely adequate preparation.

The job was, of course, too big for any one man and the service his country had created to cope with it understood this. No one man did it. Dennis, like the rest, was only part of it, as dependent upon orders from above as the men who now cursed him were dependent upon orders from him. Kane might be dead in a ditch, drunk in a boudoir, stalemated in passionate dispute with still Higher Command, or cutting his fingernails; it did not matter. He had left an order with Dennis not to send out the field order until he returned.

The whole Division knew, of course, that Dennis had kept every phone it possessed hot in his search for Kane. But, by an ethical code as strong as the order itself, it did not know and could never know that Dennis was powerless to act until he could find his superior. The Division might think what it wanted. Dennis knew the army well enough to know that it probably thought him afraid to act until he could pin responsibility on Kane, but it would never know from him the truth of why he was waiting, under a more wearing tension than any of the men who chafed around him. By the same token he realized that he himself might never know why Kane was waiting; there were always more reasons than met the eye. In the meantime he could do nothing more than wring from every minute the maximum possible preparation that could be made in the present situation and then try to set the others an example of composure and equanimity while he, too, waited. Not since the beginning of the war had he permitted himself to ponder the deeper reasons of why he waited.

Dennis had been the only son of a promising young doctor in a small Middle Western city. He had idolized the father who often played baseball with the neighborhood kids on the dusty lots and set fingers with competence and jocular reassurance in the gaslit office in their house. In the morning he was allowed to help his father into a linen duster before they started, together, the brassbound, leather-strapped car that was the wonder of the neighborhood.

As he grew older Dennis himself was allowed to open the brass petcocks and pour compounds of benzine and ether into the cylinders. They both loved the car and though Mrs. Dennis predicted with mournful pride that their experiments would blow up the whole city, they never did. Sometimes they cranked it until their arms ached; then suddenly its motor caught with resounding bursts and the doctor waved back triumphantly as he roared off at a giddy twenty miles an hour to the hospital where he was worshiped. Everywhere Dennis went, from the trackworkers' shanties down by the yard to the glittering marble edifice of the Bank, he was greeted with affection, respect, and a solicitude that warmed the casual words of the universal "How's the doc?"

Since earliest recollection his one determination had been to study medicine and practice with his father. While he was waiting for this there had been another war in which fourteen-year-old boys were not wanted. The doc had become Captain Dennis of the Medical Reserve and while they were in the first pride of his duty overseas he had been killed in a forward dressing station in the Argonne, leaving the young doctor's normal legacy of debts and good will, and a prematurely serious son.

Dennis might still have gone to medical school but he was aware of the sacrifices it would have entailed for his mother and even more aware, within himself, that the soldier had begun to overshadow the doctor in his memory of his father. When part of his heritage of good will crystallized into the offer of an appointment to the Military Academy he had accepted with a feeling of consecration.

He had become a First Classman before his expanding view had been seriously troubled by the prospect of life in a peacetime army. By then the government was offering a selected few from his class flying training.

He was fully aware that it was the uniform which had made him an aviator. It was more than a fair bargain; it was a binding pact. He was still a young man when the lucrative world of civil aviation first beckoned and then begged him greedily, but for him the decision was a simple one. The government had educated him; the obligation became all the graver with his dawning realization that only men like himself could hope to educate the government.

After that realization there had not only been no further doubts; there had been no time to doubt. Each step in his own steady progress from proficiency to eminence in an exacting profession was only a tactical victory in the interminable campaign against the entrenched tradition. The real fight was never with the finite problems of momentum and gravity but with the anachronistic power of saber and broadside. It had been a struggle to save the propeller from the sword, against the certain time when only the propeller could save the sword. But the time had come upon them with the struggle still undecided internally. Now the propellers were buying more time, at a price.

Dennis knew it was not immodesty which made him consider himself one of the few competent judges of the precariousness, the desperate uncertainty of even this bargain for time. He was one of the small earnest fraternity who had foreseen the essential outlines of this struggle long before the cries from Europe and then the thunderclap from Pearl Harbor had finally awakened even the dullest of his superiors. It was why they had sent him here, to buy them time with a minimum of the propellers for which he had worked and begged so long.

He had come with the conviction that it could be done. He had faith in the planes which carried years of his own work in most of their essential parts. He had faith in his crews and in the people from which they came, faith in the capacity of an awakened country to produce enough more planes and crews, with time.

But time was always the essence of it. His first perception of the jet plane, now panting on the threshold of operational use, had revised even his own narrow estimate of the time margin against which he was working. In this development of the jet principle he had seen and accepted a revolution that would make propellers themselves as obsolete as they had made the kind of thought that still governed them.

Realization of this had only brought him to the other side, the never-ending duality of the struggle. It was never enough to realize it; the struggle was in forcing the realization upon other people — in this case, paradoxically, upon Kane, who had been himself a legend among the pioneers for propellers. He not only had to make Kane see it, he had to make him act upon it in time. Minute by minute the decisive time, the present ephemeral gift of this favorable weather, was ticking away while his people waited for him and he, with an inner compounding of the gathering tension around him, waited for General Kane.

3

Corporal Herbert McGinnis was a victim of this general tension but he considered with more accuracy than he really knew that he was also a victim of Sergeant Evans. He had done the eight-to-four shift in the General's office and was happily contemplating his Saturday night off when he had been summoned back to fill in for Evans, who was said to be absent on a special mission for the General.

It particularly irked him because for this night McGinnis had had designs upon a newly arrived Red Cross girl in the Enlisted Men's Canteen. He had waited patiently for an hour when most of the gunners would be asleep and most of the base personnel busy. His plan had been to strike up conversation over coffee and dough-nuts and consolidate his ground with an offer to dance if that seemed tactically sound. Then when the girl had had time to realize that she could trust him he intended to sit down with her on the sofa in the ping-pong room and show her his new snapshot of Herbert McGinnis, Jr., age four months and three days.

The men in Hut Six not only had not seen the snapshot but emphatically and vocally did not want to see it. Except for this girl in the Red Cross there was no one in England who did want to see it. She, in fact, had not asked to but McGinnis had watched with green eyes the time she had spent admiring the brats of other men. He considered that it would be practically a favor to show her a kid that really did have some individuality to him. Instead he was spending his Saturday night making a computation of the Division's claims for General Dennis.

Like Evans, McGinnis was a graduate gunner, but they had little in common beside their uniforms and the service of General Dennis. McGinnis, at twenty-two, was a man of substance in his native Maryland. He had his own house, stock, implements, a half interest in forty sheep, and a hundred and sixteen acres clear. Mrs. Mc-Ginnis could and did handle a hundred and sixty turkeys a year. In addition to this gift she had brought him two cows and the ultimate certainty of her father's oystering Bugeye. The McGinnises were people who could have had a tractor loan from any bank in the county. They took more pleasure in forgoing than in possessing the tractor.

McGinnis had told the clerks at the induction center his purposes as straightforwardly as he told anyone who

111

asked. He had come to fight the enemy until he was whupped; then he was going home. It surprised him thereafter in army life to meet men who had not been sent directly to a gunnery school.

He had learned gunnery as methodically as he had once learned disking. He practiced it with the same unemotional excellence — thereby, as his last citation read, reflecting great credit upon himself and the Army Air Forces.

His social life in the army was less successful. At the end of his tour his modesty and diligence had recommended him for a job in the General's office. He had taken it with the quiet confidence of a man used to advancement in his fortunes but he got along poorly with the cynical enlisted personnel of the headquarters staff.

On operational and combat status McGinnis, like most of the others, had always been too tired to care what went on around him. With less to do he had undertaken to improve the normal level of conversation in Hut Six. The result was that the foulest mouth in Hut Six lost three teeth and McGinnis lost his hard-earned Tech stripes. He was back up to Corporal now but he still smoldered over having been demoted for decency. The sight of Evans, prospering through a career of profligacy that made McGinnis shudder for him, salted the wound. He wrote his wife that the army was deteriorating.

McGinnis was still thinking of his grievances shortly after ten that night as he worked over the General's claim board. He disliked working in the General's office itself but he knew that a man who did his duty had nothing to fear and he had been ordered to do it in there.

The General paid no more attention to him than to the furniture but it made him uncomfortable; even now he could not help overhearing every word of the General's angry voice talking over the phone: —

"I've told you four times he said he was going to visit groups and then come back here; that's all I know . . . well, tell the Embassy they don't want him any more than I do."

The phone slammed down and McGinnis started guiltily. He disliked even involuntary eavesdropping but he had begun to be interested in the frantic search for General Kane. He did not see why Dennis cared whether he found Kane or not; what was more, he did not approve. He knew that Kane was a very big wheel indeed in some remote and awful headquarters but he had run out twenty-five missions without seeing him and expected the war to be concluded on the same basis. The sages of Hut Six said that Kane spent his time undressing Duchesses and drinking tea with Ambassadors, and McGinnis felt that Dennis would do well to avoid such a man. He frowned now and industriously recrayoned a faultless number as General Dennis came over to view the board.

"How they coming, Corporal?"

"Three more destroyeds and a probable from them guys they fished out of the Channel, sir."

"Anything on that other crew in the ditch?"

"Not yet, sir. That British sub is still standing by."

"I'll be in the hole with Colonel Martin."

Dennis was gone before McGinnis could think of any way to communicate his disapproval of this unseemly concern over General Kane. He was still scowling over it when the anteroom door opened and Evans strolled in with an air of languid complacency. In spite of private resolutions McGinnis found himself speaking as he had learned to speak in the army.

"Where in hell you been?"

"Busy. Where's Dennis?"

"In the hole. You listen here, Evans . . ."

"Was he smoking?"

"No."

Evans sauntered to the General's desk, took out the cigar box, selected a cigar, and lit it. McGinnis watched with horror, half expecting to see lightning strike in the room. Instead he saw, and then smelled, only a fragrant cloud of smoke. Deep inside McGinnis something cracked; he was scarcely shocked to hear himself saying: —

"How about one of them for me?"

"He'd notice two burning," said Evans.

McGinnis continued to watch with rising fury as Evans now lifted out the whiskey bottle, measured its depleted contents with a rueful eye, and then helped himself to a short, restorative swig. He was about to burst out when Evans proffered the bottle.

"You know I never touch it. Ain't that the General's?"

"I and the General share everything," said Evans.

"Except work," said McGinnis bitterly. "I notice you share that with me; you leave it and I do it."

Evans replaced the bottle and eyed the Corporal sardonically.

"McGinnis, if there's one thing I pride myself on as a Tech Sergeant it's never doing nothing a corporal can do for me."

"You been doing some special job for Dennis?"

"Two," said Evans, "for a navigator."

"I wouldn't do nothing for no damn lieutenant."

"That's why you're still a corporal."

Evans sat down, stretched his legs comfortably up onto the map table, and regarded McGinnis with contemptuous tolerance. It comforted his present frame of mind to rediscover someone stupider than himself. Brockhurst's car had yielded another case of whiskey. From this Evans had solaced Peterson with four bottles and the locksmith with two. The division left him with a wealth that made him, for the first time since he had been in the island, uneasy about German bombers. He had hidden it beyond reach of any possible frailty in Peterson, procured the ice cream from the cook shack, and set off on his mission in the General's car with the feeling, not uncommon to affluence, that Providence does watch out for the deserving.

He had accomplished his mission at the Magruders' with what might be described as a double success and the expenditure of only half his ice cream. By nine forty-five he was free. He had the General's car, a gallon of ice cream, enough whiskey for a field marshal, part of his natural energy, a man-deserted county, and all the night left for the further benevolence of an obviously approving fate.

But regaining the car he was troubled, as he had been troubled through even the most delicate moments of his negotiations with the ladies Magruder, over what was happening to General Dennis. He had driven straight to the station and re-entered to the resounding anti-climax of finding McGinnis making crayon scores on a gaudy cardboard chart. He shook his head uneasily.

"What you got there, McGinnis?"

"Claims! Look at them lying scoundrels. Ninety-seven! If the Germans seen that they'd bust their guts laughing. How come Dennis got such a wild hair in his crotch for claims tonight?"

"Percent's riding him again," said Evans.

McGinnis remembered other things the sages of Hut Six had remarked of the biggest wheel on their horizon.

"Oh. We going to destroy that *Luftwaffe* again for this Sunday's papers?"

"With pictures," said Evans. "Full face and both stars showing."

McGinnis eyed the claim board unhappily. "I wished they'd quit this. My wife she wrote me a letter. She said in that there letter she said: 'You've done destroyed that *Luftwaffe* six times now. When you coming home?'"

"What did you tell her?"

"I didn't know *what* to tell her. I expect she thinks it's *all* lies now."

"Tell her we've beat Germany," said Evans. "Tell her we're just staying here till we outclaim MacArthur."

McGinnis pondered this. "We better hurry up then while we still got something to do it with. Eddie Cahill he called up to tell you he couldn't get to town tonight. He said he told the new C. O. over to the 641st if they ever had another day like today he was fixing to resign as line chief and take out a junk dealer's license."

"That gang ought to get their thumbs out," said Evans. "They never could fly formation."

McGinnis, remembering the truth of this from his own combat days, nodded. "They ought to do better

116

now they lost Colonel Ledgrave and Captain Jenks, though. You reckon Dennis is going to send 'em again tomorrow?"

"Maybe a milk run," said Evans. "But not no real mission till Percent's got his picture on the front of *Time* again, or *Life* anyway."

McGinnis scowled. "That's what the guys in Hut Six say. But you know it don't look right to me. If we got 'em to fight we just as well to fight 'em and get it over with. That's the way I figured my twenty-five."

"Is that why they made you a general?"

"I don't see no stars on you, Evans . . ."

McGinnis broke off just in time to manage a rigid attention as the Ops door crashed inward under the impact of the General's shoulder. McGinnis knew that nothing could save Evans now and, to his surprise, felt sorry. It wasn't right. Evans *had* stolen the General's cigar and a man who stole things . . .

"Haley!" called the General.

Without a glance at the noncoms Dennis walked in now, his eyes making a swift arc from Ops room to blackboard. Evans got himself to attention unnoticed. As Haley hurried frantically after the General to the blackboard Evans slid, with a crablike, sidling motion, to the desk and deposited the burning cigar in the General's ash tray.

"That's one forty-nine . . . now; crews?" snapped the General.

"One fifty-three, sir."

"How many would finish their tours tomorrow?"

"Fourteen, sir. Too many to spare."

Dennis shook his head wearily. "Weather?"

"No change of consequence in the twenty-two hundred, sir."

"Good. Anything else?"

Haley walked over to McGinnis and the chart now. The General returned to his desk, picked the burning cigar out of the ash tray, and inhaled with satisfaction. He looked faintly surprised as McGinnis gasped and then coughed twice.

"The claim chart is done, sir," said Haley.

With his cigar going comfortably the General moved back and scrutinized the chart attentively. Then with brief and absent thanks he dismissed McGinnis, who retired with a final glance of fury at the bland Evans. Haley shuffled the papers in his pudgy hands.

"Those medical officers are waiting, sir."

"Keep 'em," said Dennis. "Any calls?"

"Mostly for General Kane, sir. Colonel Saybold has called three times, the Embassy four more, and Lady Grattonfield six."

Unexpectedly Dennis smiled. "Any idea what they want?"

Haley had noted the smile. "I've no idea what Colonel Saybold or the Embassy want, sir."

He observed the General's appreciative grin with relief. Haley never could be sure of General Dennis; he would miss the most obvious jokes and then be observed indulging his tight-faced chuckle over things Haley did not consider funny. But this time it was all right.

Haley waited through a decorous interval and then began to shuffle the papers again when he saw that the General had forgotten him for a quizzical scrutiny of Evans, who still preserved a caricature of the faithful soldier at attention. The General drew a long puff of smoke and looked closely at his cigar.

"How did you come out, Sergeant?"

"Mission accomplished, sir," said Evans complacently.

"Not quite," said Haley.

They both looked at him in astonishment now as he drew the paper from between his second and third fingers and proceeded with relish.

"Mrs. Magruder phoned, sir, to express her apologies to her Allies and withdraw her daughter's charges . . ."

"Good," grunted Dennis. Haley could see he was chuckling inside at this but most men would not have known it.

". . . on one condition, sir. It appears that she and her daughter are lonely now that Mr. Magruder is at sea and she would like to have Sergeant Evans billeted at her house for protection."

Haley lowered the paper and turned a blank face on the General. For a second he wondered if he should have risked it. Then he saw Dennis's face tighten with severity and knew it was all right. He would have seen no expression if it was not.

"Well, I'm sure the Sergeant will volunteer for that, too."

Haley watched with satisfaction while the Sergeant reddened and hesitated perceptibly. He had seen Evans wriggle out of too many scrapes to have entire hope for this, but it looked promising.

"Sir," said Evans, "my oath was to preserve, protect, and defend the Constitution of the United States. It didn't say anything about permanent stud duty."

Dennis looked intently at the cigar in his hand while

Haley wondered, enviously, if the stories about the Magruders were true. He knew that enlisted men usually had the best luck in those matters. Something in the throaty, confident ingratiation of Mrs. Magruder's voice over the phone tonight had reminded him how long it was since he had seen Mrs. Haley.

"The United States needs navigators, Sergeant," said the General solemnly.

"Sir," said the horrified Evans, "I wouldn't do this to an admiral."

"We haven't got an admiral handy," said Dennis.

Evans was now sweating. General Dennis appeared to be taking inner satisfaction from the flinty glances which he alternated between Evans's eyes and the cigar in his hand. It would be just like that poker-faced bastard, he thought, to have caught on and to be settling the whole deal outside the book without an official word about it. On the other hand it might just be his own bad conscience. He tried to match the General's formality.

"Sir, I should like to volunteer for the Fortieth Air Army for a second tour as gunner in the Chinese theater."

"I'll sign the papers as soon as your mission here is accomplished," said Dennis. "This navigator only has ten more missions till we can get him out of here."

Joke or not, Dennis had him. Evans thought fast.

"Sir, if another man was to volunteer to substitute or at least share . . ."

"That's up to you and him as long as the . . . er . . . duty is performed satisfactorily."

"Thank you, sir," said Evans, and executing his most correct about-face he hurried into the Ops room to find McGinnis.

Haley watched Dennis's face soften suddenly and heard a quick chuckle as the door closed on Evans. Within himself he felt a deep inner glow. The joke had turned out perfectly and he still had the very cream of it to offer for their private delectation.

"There's just one more point about this, sir."

"Well . . .?"

"The navigator involved didn't get back today."

Haley saw Dennis wince, saw the life and sparkle fade into the old weary intensity of his normal face, and, too late, could have bitten his tongue off. The General turned away from him a second and then abruptly wheeled back, all business.

"Oh. Be sure to have his Group Exec go through his things personally before they're sent home, Haley."

"I've told him to, sir."

"And you'd better tell Evans it's love's labor lost" — but the brief smile was heavy now.

"Sir, he works better when he's a little tired."

"Handle it your own way. What else?"

"The boys in the groups are in a hell of a sweat to know if there'll be a mission tomorrow, sir."

"So am I. Keep 'em alerted."

"Sir, it's after ten and they want briefing poop and bomb loads. Most of 'em haven't had their clothes off for seventy-two hours."

"Neither has anyone else, except Evans." Dennis thought a minute. "Cut another field order tape using the data for Phase Two Operations Stitch."

"Phase *two*, sir?"

"That's what I said."

Haley saw that deep fatigue had repossessed Dennis.

But in their entire time together he had never known the General to make a mistake like this. He coughed and spoke diffidently.

"Sir, I understood that General Kane had said . . ."

"I didn't say to put it on the printer. I said to cut the tape."

The voice rasped. Haley stiffened reflexively and made for the door without a word. He had almost reached it when a softer accent stopped him: —

"Ernie . . ."

He turned to see Dennis striding toward him, his face relaxed and his voice contrite under its fatigue.

"I'm sorry. I'm tired."

It gave Haley one of the bitterest moments he had known in service. He had not only bothered his chief with a joke that misfired; he had behaved like a petulant child over a well-earned rebuke. He had to gulp before he was sure he could speak without intruding further emotion into Dennis's troubles.

"Roger, sir. You ought to get some sleep, Casey."

Dennis smiled wryly and clapping Haley on the shoulder walked into the Ops room with him.

Chapter Seven

EVANS HAD BARELY cornered McGinnis in the Ops room when he noticed the hurried passage of Dennis and Haley through it on their way down to the hole. Leading the suspicious Corporal back into the relative privacy of the General's office, Evans took out the cigar box, opened it, and extended it with a hospitable smile.

"What you after now, Evans?"

"I'm fixing to share things more with you," said Evans.

"What else we sharing?"

Evans snapped the box shut, replaced it with a fine simulation of indifference, and shrugged his shoulders.

"Okay, if you want to be a corporal all your life."

McGinnis looked regretfully after the vanishing cigars and thought of his lost Tech stripes. The world was certainly askew but Evans seemed to have it firmly under control.

"What you bucking for now?" he inquired more cordially.

"Dennis won't let me go to China till I've got someone to take my place. It's worth Tech stripes but if you don't want it . . ."

"What's the catch in this?"

"Security."

"*Security!*" Evans averted his eyes from the outraged face and judged the progressive results of this remark by the almost discernible rise in the Corporal's temperature.

"Security hell! I never told no one nothing yet!"

"You never heard nothing yet. In this job you hear the truth about things they don't tell the President. Would you be willing to live off the station, away from the other boys?"

"For Tech stripes? I'd be glad to get away from them boys a while just to *be* away. I'm so sick of hearing them talk about just that one thing . . ."

"I know," said Evans gravely. "It's disgusting. Well, there's some people want a respectable soldier to live there for protection . . ."

They both jumped to silent attention as Dennis, with one of his habitually unexpected appearances, walked back in, made straight for his desk, and sitting down pulled out the Jenks file. Evans winked at McGinnis, who scuttled silently out.

Alone, Evans studied the General forgivingly. The joke, if it was one, was now being projected down the hierarchy in traditional style with the most promising prospects. And if Dennis had known about the cigars his behavior had been generous.

"Excuse me, sir. You had any chow yet?"

"I'm expecting General Kane."

"He'd be pretty stringy, sir. I'll get you something."

He thought he saw a swift glow of gratitude in the General's bleak face as he went out.

Martin, entering the General's office quietly a few minutes later, had a more detached look at his friend than he had thought of taking for years. Dennis was standing with a personnel file in his hand, looking back and forth between those black dots on the map and the file itself in a posture of ineffable weariness.

Studying him now with some of the acute attentiveness he normally preserved for the observation of engines, he wondered how Dennis took it. To ask the same question about himself would never have occurred to him. Martin had spent twenty of the last forty hours with entire aerial responsibility for the fate and effectiveness of a hundred and forty bombers through the two toughest missions of the war, to date. Sixteen of these hours he had been on oxygen, three of them he had spent shooting a machine gun for his life in the nose of a crippled Fort. He was thinking now that, as always in their long relationship, Dennis had the tough job.

Dennis, of course, was an Academy man and he liked the service; at least he had liked it once. There had been times during the latter years when Martin had begun to wonder about that. His own views of the service were so simple they had made a legend. At the reception after his graduation from flying school, the benign old colonel who had suffered most through Martin's training had asked the newly created lieutenant what he thought of the uniform now.

"Just what I always thought, sir. It stinks, but you have nice airplanes."

Martin had been demoted three times before reaching his captaincy. In his official file, however, there had long been established separate subcategories, a C for citations and commendations and an R for reprimands. The balance between these two had kept him almost abreast of classmates who had their first of either to earn.

He would not have cared if it hadn't. To Martin the

uniform was simply an inconvenience attendant upon life in a world full of airplanes no impecunious young man could hope to own. He considered it a fair bargain.

At his peak there were not half a dozen Americans who could fly in the same sky with him. Dennis, already declining a little with the inevitable slowing up of the thirties, had been the only one of these in uniform. They had lived and worked and flown and played together for fifteen years. It was Dennis who had twice kept Martin in the service through crises the Citation and Commendation file might not have balanced.

When Dennis had been given the Fifth Division his first personnel request had been for Martin. It had troubled his conscience at the time because he had known what Martin could do, perhaps should be doing, for the teething troubles of the B–29's. On the other hand he had known the kind of thing Martin would and did do under most commanders. The Fifth Division was an Operational Command; its priority was clear. Only the coincidence of his overpowering personal inclination kept Dennis pondering the matter several days before deciding as he wished.

For Martin himself there had never been the slightest indecision about what he was going to do. He was grateful that Dennis's good sense had finally saved them both the trouble of having him desert some other command to join the Fifth. It would have taken a lot of fixing.

Studying Dennis now as he pondered the Jenks file, unaware of anything else, Martin felt a hot, futile indignation. It was this kind of waste effort, this pressure for which there were no gauges, that was slowly, visibly doing things to Dennis that momentum and gravity and centrifugal force had never been able to do. Martin could feel immeasurable weight on that fragile form, weight he could not share.

It filled him with a sudden fury, not against Jenks but against the whole irrational structure that could let things like that consume Dennis. Toward Jenks himself Martin had no feeling. He knew him for a poor pilot but plenty of those got through. To ground such a man in combat was to issue a tacit invitation to malingerers. But if Jenks preferred the risk of quitting to running out six more missions it was probably a break for the crews who would have ridden with him.

He was pondering how to say this so as to comfort Dennis when Dennis himself looked up, bleakly at first, and then with the quick smile that always welcomed his recognition of Martin.

"Find it?"

The question, confronting Martin again with his own failure of that afternoon, swept the whole Jenks affair out of his mind.

"Not in the first three categories. Jake's working out the target folders on the fourth now. Found our wandering General?"

"No."

"He must have heard of another camera somewhere."

Dennis grunted but said nothing. They had long since effected a tacit compromise on these matters. Dennis never rebuked Martin's habitual insubordinations when they were in private. Martin never allowed his tongue or attitude to embarrass Dennis in public. At the moment, however, he wanted above all things to get Dennis away from his troubles for respite if he could. There were few things that would divert him but his own sympathy was one of them.

"Casey, did Cliff say anything about Helen?"

"He says she's worried."

Dennis tossed the Jenks file on the desk now, to indicate his receptiveness if Martin wished to speak of this matter. He rarely did and latterly only with the shrugging indifference that indicated by itself the tragic finality of it. Tonight, however, he appeared to have it on his mind and Dennis listened with concentration.

"Worried about me or the kid?"

"You."

"She always was — and with reason. I guess I was a pretty harebrained kid."

He mused a second and it was too long. Involuntarily Dennis's eyes had gone back to the map. The glance returned Martin abruptly to the implacable present. He spoke half bitterly.

"Now I'm Eagle-eye Martin — sure death on any target below the first three categories."

"Quit hurting," said Dennis sharply. "You've had this coming. It's averages."

"Not with Cliff here," said Martin. "Why couldn't he stay with the United Chiefs? He wore his lips out getting there."

He waited but Dennis deliberately evaded.

"Ted, are you and Helen going to click this time?"

Martin shrugged. "Maybe. I guess she didn't feel so secure on her own, either. I won't be flying forever. You know the thing that pulled my ripcord with the whole Garnett family was turning down that airline job."

128

"Twelve thousand a year is a lot of dough for a kid to laugh off."

"I heard you turn down eighteen the same day, Grandpa. But those Garnetts always worshiped security, I guess because they'd been army so long. At heart the guy's jealous of us."

"He's done well, Ted."

"At staff work."

"We had to have those guys to get planes for hoodlums like you and me," said Dennis easily.

"Maybe," Martin smiled fleetingly. "Helen tried everything in the book to make me one of 'em — indoors, flying tail cover on Cliff's desk. She figures he's a cinch for the top someday."

"She's probably right," said Dennis slowly.

It always came to this, Martin reflected. He and Casey would find a few unexpected minutes together and it would be almost like the old days. Then, no matter what they were talking about, their new troubles closed in on them. It was so now and he knew he had to make the most of this time for the newest and nearest of them.

"Casey, she's right except for one thing. No record will be worth a damn after this war without Combat Command in it. Cliff knows that. And this is still the best air command in the war."

"Maybe it is, until the B-29's come along."

"They're still a dream, maybe a nightmare. Cliff always follows the beaten tracks, at a safe distance."

Dennis smiled. "Ted, you're imagining things."

Martin jumped up and thumped the Swastika on the wall.

"I'm not imagining that. These things are going to be

129

more fun than adultery, for the guys who have them. I admit I'd hate to see Cliff get your job but I'd hate it worse to see Galland get these before we get our new fighters."

"So would I," said Dennis. He was not smiling now.

"Well, he will if you tell Kane about today *now*. But if he thinks we're two-thirds done we can probably brace his spine enough to let us finish Fendelhorst tomorrow."

"And after that?"

"*After that* we discover today's mistake. He'll be in so deep by then he'll have to finish to justify himself. Those pictures will keep him happy for twenty-four hours more. My God, Casey, they're fooling the experts down in the hole and Kane doesn't know a strike photo from a Wassermann. Why do you have to tell him tonight?"

"Why did you tell me?"

"I could trust you."

Dennis considered before speaking slowly: "He trusts us, Ted."

Martin exploded into blasphemy and then checked it. He knew that all the profanity at his command would not dent the rocky scruple in Dennis. He had to use reason, and he had to do it fast, while there was time. He was wondering how much time he had when General Kane himself walked through the door.

Toward Kane Martin felt only the essential contempt he cherished for all things military. He had long since recognized that the caste system was more than a relic of the monarchical principle to which armies clung so wistfully. It was vital armor against reason or competition. Toward Kane's rank Martin felt no more respect than toward any other, including his own.

As a young man Martin had revered Kane's flying record. As a maturing pilot he had realized that Kane's private compass had always been set for the kind of stars men wear. He observed now that Kane was traveling with a characteristic retinue. Besides his distinguished visitor he had brought one aide and one newspaperman. Martin accepted the introductions quietly in his turn, offered an indifferent hand to his brother-in-law, and nodded absently to Garnett's compliments on the mission and his eager insistence upon a good private talk later on.

His mind was on Dennis. He listened to Kane's explanations that the party had extended its visiting to the headquarters of General Endicott's neighboring division and had felt obliged to stop there for dinner. Dennis appeared to him to have shed both fatigue and tension. He looked as calm and self-possessed as if they were about to settle to cards. So did Kane.

"There are some messages for you, sir," Dennis was saying.

"Anything from Washington?"

"No, sir."

"They can wait."

The bell had rung but even Martin was unprepared for the immediacy of Dennis's opening.

"Sir, may I speak with you briefly, alone?"

"Of course, Casey. But first I want Cliff to tell you . . ."

"Sir, may I have one minute alone with you?"

Kane was not used to being interrupted. He spoke shortly.

"All night, when you've heard what I want you to

hear. Cliff, will you tell Casey what we decided?"

It was Garnett, rather than Dennis, who now showed embarrassment over this superficial discourtesy of Kane's, but an order was an order. After a hesitant glance at Brockhurst and Prescott, who had drawn a little away from the faint turbulence now making itself felt in the room, he plunged in.

"Casey, I felt it was impossible for you people to be doing anything so serious without informing higher authority."

"That's why I filed a report and recommendations."

Martin locked his face muscles against the involuntary grin. He had seen Kane quicken with the impact of the remark. He knew it was no inadvertence that had caused Dennis to make it. The next job probably wouldn't be as good as this one but Casey would be the same guy in it instead of a different man clinging to this one. For the first time he felt a twinge of pity for Garnett's evident unease. But as Kane chose to default the retort by silence, Garnett had to continue.

"Well, Casey, they never reached us. So General Kane and I have been talking to Washington by tele-print conversation from Joe Endicott's. We felt we owed it to the Chief to put him in the position of being able to defend what we . . . what's being done here, if he approves it. Brockie here was good enough to write the whole thing out for us so as to put it in the most forceful and favorable light. I think if you'll read it . . ."

He nodded to Brockhurst, who stepped forward now and offered Dennis a roll of teletype paper. Dennis had heard the news with a sense of lifting relief that the

132

information had at last reached levels of authority commensurate with its importance. Garnett's action had put the thing in its proper position, bringing the essence of the army's strength, which was its unity, to bear upon it.

"I've read enough of Brockhurst's lily-gilding. What did the Chief say?"

"Unfortunately he's in Florida, at the proving grounds."

"Testing a new typewriter?"

"General!" said Kane. "I can't tolerate such remarks. The Chief's public relations policy has put us where we are today."

"It sure has," said Dennis.

Garnett intervened hastily. "We had a very constructive talk with Lester Blackmer, Casey. You know how close Les and the Chief are."

"I know," said Dennis. "What did Lester Yessir say?"

"Well, he couldn't speak officially but he's sure the Chief will be 100 per cent behind us in principle."

Evans, entering with a trayful of sandwiches just then, blessed the luck that had brought him back at this minute. The room was crackling with tension. Kane's face was now a dull brick red. Dennis had his jaw locked on a dead cigar but Evans could tell from the exaggerated levelness of his voice that he was angry.

"These gentlemen have eaten, Sergeant."

"Do they know you haven't, sir?"

Kane saved Evans the rebuke he had fully expected by turning quickly to Dennis with courteous solicitude.

"I'm sorry, Casey. Put those things on the table, Sergeant. We'll be going soon."

"That's fine, sir," said Evans blandly. Moving to the

map table he cocked his ears and began unloading as slowly as he dared.

"Les warned us, Casey," continued Garnett, "that the Chief may be very upset about our . . . your losses. He said he'd help us by working up a big feature story on claims . . ."

"Did you get those added up, General?" asked Kane.

"Multiplied, sir." Dennis pointed dryly to the gaudy claim chart and Kane hurried to it for a personal inspection.

"Les will also stress the importance of these targets when he can reach the Chief and . . ." they all felt Garnett hesitate . . . "he's going to try to sell the Chief on letting us finish *after the allocation meeting*."

Dennis walked straight over to Kane, who kept his eyes on the chart.

"Sir, did you let that little two-star stooge forbid our mission for tomorrow?"

The phrasing of the question deflected Kane's mind from its manifest insubordination. It was all very well for Dennis to dismiss Blackmer so contemptuously. Kane knew that no major general got that close to the Chief for the purpose of dulling his knives on brigadiers. Blackmer was his own contemporary. Kane had had a bad moment on learning who would steer the report of this situation to the Chief. He answered testily, as much to his own worries as to Dennis's open anger.

"Of course not. If there's one thing the Chief prides himself on it's not letting his own people interfere with his commanders' freedom of action in the field."

Dennis caught himself quickly. "That's fine, sir. Now the groups are waiting for the order and . . ."

"Not so fast, Casey. Les indicated to us, unofficially, that it would be a great thing to put the Chief in a position to announce a new monthly record for sorties and tonnages just before that meeting on Tuesday."

"We can't take record tonnages that far, sir."

"I'm afraid that's the point," said Garnett. "Les virtually promised us if we'd take things easy for the last two days of this month he thought everything would be all right with the Chief after Tuesday."

"Including weather, I suppose . . . in Washington."

"Casey, you'll get weather again," said Garnett soothingly.

"When?" demanded Dennis. "I've waited five weeks for this. Twice we had one day; this job takes three. If we ever do get them again the big wheels will be after us for headlines over those subpens or tearing up the French perfume trade to discourage the Italians or covering some State Department four flush in the Balkans — any other damned thing on the planet except the one thing that will decide whether American bombardment can stay in business at all."

Martin was finding it hard work to cover his excitement. He did not see how even Kane could have let the argument go on so far if his mind were made up. If it were not there was a chance, almost too elusive for measurement, but present still in the wavering course of this discussion. It lay in Kane himself, in the irresolution which was still permitting Garnett to carry the preliminary skirmish for him while he studied it and calculated. Garnett seemed to be sensing his superior's uncertainty; he continued persuasively.

"Casey, we know you've had distractions. Nobody

135

can take all the politics out of war. But you don't need three days again. As Lester said, the saving grace of the situation is that you're two thirds done. . . ."

He broke off with annoyance, looking toward the door, and Martin, following his gaze, saw with dismay that Lieutenant Jake Goldberg had burst wildly into the room, his arms laden with maps and photos and target folders.

3

Goldberg had crashed through the door with the velocity of flight. He was fleeing from himself. For on the way upstairs from the laboratory in the hole he had paused briefly to think for the first time since his eyes had seen the target folder in his hands superimpose, line for line, over the photos on the light table and his feet had started instantly for the General's office.

His brief pause en route he now saw as the darkest of moral compromises. It had occurred to him that there was some comfort in what he had learned. At least the thing wasn't a hospital.

Goldberg was a boy who understood the cost of the advantages that had been given him. His mother and father kept a delicatessen just off Santa Monica Boulevard. From their cash till Goldberg had been sent through all of high school and two years of college. His brain had been as immediately and happily at home with trig and calculus as the others around him were with jockies' records and dance tunes. Goldberg's parents had seen for the boy a chance beyond their own horizons.

War changed the chance; he was graduated number

one in a class of six hundred bombardiers to become an officer in the Army of the United States. He had learned. He had been ready, equipped, and useful when his country wanted him.

Then, in one day, he had not only mistaken a target which was important enough to take the Division beyond fighters, he had found himself on the verge of trying to ameliorate his failure in the eyes of General Dennis and Colonel Martin by misrepresenting, with considered words, the importance of what he had hit.

This afternoon, as soon as the photos had come in, General Dennis had come down to the light table instead of sending for them. Before looking at them he had cleared his throat and said: "Goldberg, Colonel Martin has told me this is not your fault. He still thinks you're the best bombardier in the army and he's the best judge I know. Now find out what you did hit and bring it to me at once."

The officers in the conference looked up at his intrusion with astonishment. They saw an unshaven lieutenant, face still grimy from powder smoke, eyes red from strain and tears. His proximity to acute hysteria was apparent in everything but the inflexible steadiness of purpose with which he now thrust his maps and photos straight at General Dennis, oblivious of everyone else in the room.

"I've found the damned thing, sir," he said.

Only then did he look around to see a Major General, another Brigadier, and two strangers gaping at his appearance.

"Excuse me, sir . . . You said . . ."

"That's right," said Dennis quickly. "General Kane, this is today's lead bombardier, Lieutenant Goldberg."

Kane had had time to study the boy's condition. He stepped forward now and extended his hand with benign paternalism.

"Good evening, Lieutenant. That was a wonderful mission you boys ran today. I couldn't wait to see the pictures myself but I've been talking to a member of the Big Chief's personal staff and he says the Chief will be very proud of you."

Goldberg accepted the handshake absently. His mind was still on the folders in his other hand. To his astonishment it was Colonel Martin who grabbed him by the arm and started him toward the door, speaking quickly to Kane.

"Very sorry you were interrupted, sir. This can wait."

He was propelling Goldberg forcibly toward the door when General Kane himself saw the pictures and, reaching out, took them out of the Lieutenant's hand. At the first glance his face began to beam.

"Look, Cliff, look. These are wonderful. . . . You see . . . here's the highway coming in, here's the river, here's the factory . . ."

Free from Martin, Goldberg stepped over to the General now, his mind clear again and focused entirely on the pictures.

"You've got them upside down, General," he said.

Major Prescott wondered for an instant whether he should put this unspeakable Lieutenant in his place. But keeping his mouth shut, Prescott walked over to join his senior's admiration of the photographs. It was Dennis who spoke now, very sharply, but not to Goldberg.

"General Kane, may I have a minute alone with you?"

This time Kane did show his irritation openly.

"I've told you, General, you can have all night, as soon as we're done. Look, Cliff! Look at that blast here on the smoke fringe." He stopped, cogitated, and then spoke with decision. "These will have to go to the Chief at once by special plane."

"Sir," said Major Prescott. "Considering the importance of these I should like permission to work up a special presentation of them . . . frame them dramatically on good white board . . . using before and after shots, with a title, 'The Death of Schweinhafen.' "

Kane beamed. "The very thing, Homer, the very thing."

"It isn't Schweinhafen," said Lieutenant Goldberg.

"Not Schweinhafen . . . what is it?" Kane glared.

"The Nautilus Torpedo plant at Gritzenheim, sir."

"Torpedo plant . . . ?" echoed Kane.

Garnett's reflexes were faster. He had seized the photos now and his face lit up at the new examination of them.

"General, this couldn't be more opportune. The Admirals will want to see this. If we can get these to the Big Chief before that meeting . . ."

Kane got it now. He beamed upon Goldberg and then, as his whole perception expanded, he clapped the Lieutenant affectionately upon the shoulder.

"I'll send my own plane. Lieutenant, you don't know what this will do for us. When we can show our commanders that in the midst of the greatest air campaign in history we still think enough of the overall strategy to knock out a torpedo factory too . . ."

"I'm sorry, sir," said Dennis. "We hit it by accident instead of Schweinhafen."

139

Chapter Eight

GENERAL KANE understood what had happened at once. In all the world, he thought, there was no man who had luck like this. Nothing new. Just a fresh instance of the kind of thing that dogged him interminably. The thought of how the Germans must be laughing at him was bitter.

The Germans could afford to laugh. They had everything, over there; a short defense perimeter and impenetrable weather to reduce even the simplified problem of defending their economy with flak and policing it with swarms of cheap, expendable fighters. They had a docile, industrious people, a press that knew its place, no congress, no allies, and a leader who loved war and warriors.

They had even had the whole Spanish campaign for maneuvers and testing. Kane's contemporaries in the Reich had had an easy and profitable dress rehearsal for the whole war. The men who had gone down there had gained practical experience, advanced three or four ranks in a season, and come home to permanent promotion, decorations, and adulation.

He thought of them bitterly — Kesselring, Lohr, Von Griem, Sperrle, Stumpf, Galland, Richthofen, Jeschonnek, Harlinghausen . . . he had met many of them in Berlin on a brief observation tour before the war. He had stayed in a cheap hotel and pondered the problem of squeezing taxi fares out of what his government thought a suitable per diem, while these men flashed through the Kurfürstendamm and down the Unter den Linden in their sleek black Mercedes cars which the police saluted.

He shook his head heavily now, aware of the tightening silence through which the other men were regarding him. He had to deal with this now, somehow; it was always this way. There was never time. Turning to Dennis he spoke slowly, warily, half fearful still of further and worse disclosures waiting behind that expressionless face.

"You told me you'd destroyed Schweinhafen."

"It was a mistake, sir. We hit this Nautilus place."

"Whose mistake?"

"Mine, sir. The preparatory instruction . . ."

"No, you don't," said Martin. "The briefing was perfect. I led the Division and I loused it up myself, General Kane."

Goldberg broke in. "These gentlemen are both covering for me, sir. I was well briefed and I was on the sight. It's my fault, sir. I just got mixed up in the fighting."

It was too much. Kane could feel himself giving way again to anger.

"Why did you *get* mixed up? Were you scared?"

"Yes, sir. I'm always scared but . . ."

The fool would talk all night if permitted. Kane wheeled on Dennis.

"This *is* your fault, General, entrusting a mission of this importance to a bombardier who . . ."

"General Kane, Lieutenant Goldberg is on the fourth

141

mission of a voluntary second tour over German targets. You owe him an apology."

Glancing back and forth now between the deepening purple of Kane's anger and the white-faced intensity of Dennis, Evans began to realize what was happening to him. As Brockhurst had warned that afternoon, he was going to see a general fired. At the first suggestion of the idea he had relished it. Now he realized that Dennis was fighting in his own way, and within limitations, everything that Evans himself hated about the army, fully conscious of the risk as he took it. What was more, he was fighting capably. And now Goldberg addressed Dennis with quiet composure through the ominous deepening silence of Kane.

"It's all right, sir. General Kane just doesn't understand."

"I understand," said Kane icily, "that you've made a fool of me and the Army Air Forces, letting us report that we've destroyed a target we didn't even touch. This could embarrass the Chief. Do you realize what I'd be justified in doing?"

"Yes, sir. You ought to shoot me for wasting the lives of four hundred and eighteen men this afternoon. I'd be grateful if you did."

Without saluting, Goldberg turned and walked out the Ops room door. Kane was still staring, as incredulously as the others, when he heard Brockhurst speaking. The words came to him as if from very far away but they were clear.

"I think I'd take it easy on that one, R. G."

Brockhurst had not intended to intervene. It was costing him an increasing effort to remain either neutral or silent.

What met the eye was two exhausted men compressed to the combustion point by the weight of command. Brockhurst himself could not be sure yet of the merits of the argument. He could be and was appalled by the process of the solution unfolding before him.

Brockhurst knew that both Kane and Dennis were widely considered to be, at their differing levels of operation, the best that the army could produce. He had not interrupted the argument to protect Goldberg. What he had feared was that the passion of either Kane or Dennis might explode.

It warmed his sympathy to see that Martin was already working for the same purpose. Ordinarily the Colonel was almost openly contemptuous of Kane. Now he was addressing him as if he had never cursed a commander in his life.

". . . and I know the boy spoke out of turn, sir. But he isn't our Division bombardier by accident. He made the best patterns in his school, his squadron, his group, and his wing. He volunteered for this second tour of German targets only because he knows how much we need him. He knows how much the Germans would like to get their hands on him, too. The mistake was *my* fault, General. It was rugged out there and I couldn't get off the nose gun for more than seconds. Jake threw a perfect pattern just where I told him to while I was standing all over his hands on the sight, shooting."

Kane had had time to regain his temper. He nodded now and his voice was warm with friendly curiosity.

"You were shooting yourself, Ted?"

Martin grinned and the whole room seemed to relax.

"Four boxes, sir. Those Krauts must have had an order for nothing but frontals today."

Prescott, noting Kane's interest, spoke earnestly.

"May I ask how many you got, sir?"

"Who could tell in a mess like that?"

"You're being modest, sir. How many did you report at the interrogation?"

"I didn't go to it."

"It might be important, sir. How many do you think?"

Martin remembered that this was giving Dennis time to cool off.

"Well, three I was shooting at came apart but I guess every top turret and nose gun in our element was working on 'em too."

Prescott stepped over and turned the claim board toward Kane.

"Three more would make an even hundred, sir, our first. In the circumstances today's claim report and battle damage should be especially carefully done, sir."

"They certainly must, Homer," said General Kane.

Prescott eyed his watch. "There would still be time for a correction to make the Sunday papers at home, sir."

"Correction on claims, you mean?"

"Of course, sir. One hundred."

Kane pondered a minute. "Round numbers always sound suspicious, Homer. Make it a hundred and one. General Dennis, can you provide Homer and Brockie here with a place to write a press release?"

Too late, Brockhurst realized that he often under-

144

estimated Kane. With his head cool the General was as clever a man as he had known. He spoke out bluntly.

"General, are you manipulating me out of here?"

"Brockie," said Kane, "you have my promise. I need help from you now."

"Evans," said Dennis, "get these gentlemen what they need."

He walked over and held open the door himself with obvious relief as the Sergeant followed Brockhurst and Prescott out.

2

"General," said Kane, "this is very serious."

"I tried to tell you before, sir."

Kane could feel the compressed anger in the retort and he regretted having aroused it. He had half decided to relieve Dennis but it was not a thing to do precipitately. A change now would run through the whole structure with seismic dislocation. If he requested Garnett, who would get Garnett's job with the United Chiefs? Who would get whatever impending job had placed Garnett in such a manifestly intermediate position? Kane knew he could probably precalculate the chain of changes but he needed time with his most private card index.

"Ted, how many men in the Division know this?"

"Not many, sir. Most of the camera ships were lost or shot up. Both recce planes are unreported today. Most of the men were too busy fighting to care where we were."

"For all they knew you might have had a signal recalling you or changing the target en route, mightn't you?"

"I might but I didn't," said Martin.

"Cliff, do you think it's fair to the Chief, in the circumstances, to report this immediately?"

"I'd have to think that over, sir," Garnett evaded.

"We haven't much time to think," said Kane. "Sending the Chief into that meeting with this hanging over him is practically sabotage. I reported a successful strike to Lester in good faith. Ted admits that even he was mixed up. There won't be confirmatory recce for a couple of days. We could use them to put the Chief in a very strong position."

"Yes, we could finish the job," said Dennis thoughtfully.

"Casey! Half the United Chiefs are admirals. Naval objectives are a legitimate . . ."

"This one was Fourth Category," said Dennis bluntly.

"They don't know individual targets on that level," snapped Kane. "This is a significant contribution to the Naval War. If we use the remaining two days of this month on naval objectives *under fighter cover* we can average down losses, set new sortie and tonnage records, and put the navy under obligation to the Chief just before that meeting."

"And that would be the end of Stitch," said Dennis.

"Casey, today could be the end of daylight bombardment."

"*Could be*. The Germans' first good day with jets will be."

This time Kane covered his annoyance. If Dennis's years as a test pilot had not taught him that flexibility survives where rigidity breaks, that was his misfortune. But the moment for breaking stress was not yet at hand. Kane wanted time to consider it without the pressure of those six eyes and ears measuring everything he said. He smiled.

"Casey, let's take these pictures down to your light table. We'll rejoin you in a minute, gentlemen."

3

Ted Martin had realized that a private session with Garnett was unavoidable. His brother-in-law honestly thought other people's difficulties could always be resolved by a good heart-to-heart talk, with himself doing most of the talking. Through the earlier quarrels and reconciliations Ted had endured such talks attentively, hopefully. Now they were powerless to penetrate the indifference which had closed like scar tissue over the old pain. As the departure of the others locked them together again Martin amused himself by beating his brother-in-law to the punch.

"Well, how do you like life in a military bucket shop?"

The question threw Garnett off balance. He always forgot, between their meetings, Martin's disconcerting bluntness.

"Ted, how long has Casey been like this?"

"Like what?"

"So tense, strung-up, unreasonable?"

"It's a tense job. Were you sent here to replace him?"

"I don't know. It occurred to me, of course. The orders just said 'Visit Fifth Bombardment Division for

147

Tour of Observation.' It was very unexpected. Unfortunately I couldn't see the Chief personally before leaving because he was in a meeting with some very important people from Hollywood."

"What does Percent think?"

"Percent?"

"Kane."

Garnett smiled. "Between ourselves he asked me confidentially if I'd been sent here to replace him."

"Jesus! You haven't done anything bad enough to get a second star, have you?"

This time Garnett had to force the smile but he managed it.

"The same old rebel, Ted."

"What's Percent jittering about, Cliff? Is Washington onto him?"

"You know how the Chief is, Ted. He likes to keep 'em guessing."

Martin sat down on the map table, took out cigarettes, lit one, and then returned them to his pocket without offering Garnett one. He inhaled and blew out a long cloud of smoke before nodding somberly.

"I know. And then he wonders why he can't get the truth out of them. Well, they can learn it from Casey now . . . or wait about sixty days and learn it from Galland."

"Ted, why in God's name didn't you tell us before?"

"Casey tried to, through channels. But the channels between us and you are clogged up with homemade statistics these days."

"Why do you think Kane sat on the report?"

Martin smoked thoughtfully, but made no reply.

Garnett took out a cigarette of his own and lit it slowly. Nothing would change Ted's views about the army.

"Ted, you shouldn't be flying missions."

"My insurance is paid up."

"I don't mean that. Helen's worried about you."

"Lots of girls are worried. How's she coming with the kid?"

"It would ease her mind to know that you're not flying."

"I haven't told her I am."

"She knows you; you wouldn't promise not to."

"Did she ask you to work me over like this?"

"You've done more than your share," said Garnett. "Think of those years before the war."

"Somebody had to do that, too."

Garnett paused. He was always finding himself on the defensive with Martin and he knew it was probably his own fault.

"Ted, I know you and Casey think because I don't wear my wings to bed the way you do I don't understand air problems. But flying isn't the only part of this; it's only the part for young men. The army needs your experience."

"The way they needed it at Dayton?"

"Ted, the Chief knows now that you were right. But the whole Board heard you tell Lester he was an opinionated goddamned ignoramus. That just isn't the way to get things done."

"What have they done with that lousy plane since? Killed a lot of kids for nothing. Casey and I told 'em six years ago it wouldn't fly if they amended the law of gravity. This is the same thing, Cliff. Now we're beginning to get good bombardment from Casey and kids like Goldberg, in spite of those old bastards. This time they haven't got either the guts or the sense to use it for anything but political logrolling with the navy."

"Washington isn't a bowl of cherries, Ted. But changes are coming, big changes and a lot of advancement."

Martin laughed. "I bet. If you guys can keep this going long enough there ought to be three stars shining on every ring."

Garnett controlled himself. It was useless to argue and his time was short.

"We're outgrowing that, Ted. And you've got a lot of fine service behind you."

Martin studied him more closely. Most of his mind had been on Dennis and Stitch. He realized that he should have known all this palaver was Cliff's way of coming at something important, to him.

"Which way are you changing, Cliff?"

"Frankly, old man, I'm not sure. Nothing's settled yet but I have reason to think the Chief has confidence in me, and big B-29 jobs are coming up soon, jobs that will start with two stars. The commanders will pick their own chiefs of staff and they're a cinch for brigadiers to start. Think it over, boy."

Martin laughed. "Me, a chief, with all those papers?"

"Adjutants do that. But if the Chief knew I could add your operational experience to my knowledge of — er, higher echelon procedure, it would wrap it up. He remembers you."

"He should." Martin grinned impenitently.

"Well, he admires guts."

Through the blackout curtain on the window now they suddenly heard a protesting spasm of coughing barks from the tuning of some near-by recalcitrant motor. Inwardly Garnett cursed the distraction. Martin tensed, ears up, forehead furrowed, until slowly the spasm settled into a smooth, muted droning. Then, with a quick shake of his head, he looked back at Garnett.

"Thanks, Cliff, but as long as Casey will have me . . ."

"Ted, he knows there's nothing for you here as his A 3 but those same eagles. He'd release you. Casey isn't selfish."

"He'd make me go but . . ."

"We'd be a perfect team," urged Garnett. "I'd fight the navy and you could fight the Japs. Think it over and for God's sake quit this flying. There's no sense throwing yourself away when by waiting a little . . ."

"The Krauts aren't waiting, Cliff."

"Ted, there'll be good jobs in the Jap war when this one's washed up." He saw Martin's quick smile and hurried. "And those B-29's are going to be sweet."

Martin bit, hard. "What have they done about that frame expansion, Cliff?"

"They're getting it. I'll tell you the whole story later. But I want you to think about this."

"Have you spoken to Casey?"

"Not yet but . . ."

"Well, don't till I think it over or the whole deal's off. Now, what else does Helen want?"

"She wants you to pick a godfather for the impending heir."

151

"Who?"

"Well, we've talked about it but of course she wants your views, too. The doctor thinks it will be a boy. R. G. Kane will be a name to conjure with someday, Ted. He's always been fond of Helen and it would be especially appropriate if it happens while you're still here."

"I'll think it over," said Martin shortly.

"Think it all over, boy."

Chapter Nine

FROM A VANTAGE POINT in the Ops room Evans watched Kane and Dennis pass on their way back from the light table to the Brigadier's office. One glance showed him that the dispute had not been settled. Evans followed them into the office.

"The man doesn't live who could tell those pictures apart," Kane was saying.

"Preliminary twenty-three hundred serviceability, sir," said Evans.

He had seen Dennis drop his wife's letters for this as quickly as he now turned from Kane to the board. He could almost feel the intensity of those eyes on the hand with which he chalked the figures up. Stealing a glance around he saw with indignation that the others were making free of Dennis's cigars, but the General had eyes only for his board.

"One twenty-six . . . that's fine."

"Them guys on the line really got their fingers out tonight, sir."

"And they're still promising twenty-three more in time for bomb loading?"

It had been a rule of Evans's army career never to volunteer information. But he had broken several of his own rules today already. Again he had it in his power to assuage some of the anxiety in Dennis.

"Twenty-five, sir."

153

He was rewarded by a fleeting smile. "Oh . . . twenty-*five!* Thank Cahill for me, Sergeant."

"Sir, them officers are still waiting."

"Let 'em sleep while they wait, but keep 'em."

As Evans made for the Ops room he had a further reward in the cool self-possession of the voice Dennis now addressed to General Kane: "Sir, we've got the planes and the weather. The people at the groups are waiting for the order. . . ."

In the doorway itself, however, Evans had to stand aside for the hurried passage of Prescott and Brockhurst.

Inside the office Kane looked up at the interruption with obvious relief. Swallowing his annoyance, Dennis observed now that Brockhurst was looking disturbed and skeptical, his forehead creased with a heavy frown. Prescott, however, had taken on a new animation. His face glowed with the happy flush of creative endeavor.

"General Kane, I think this time I can promise you something really good. I borrowed some of General Dennis's draftsmen and I'm having them make three-by-five mountings for the panels, flat white board with glossy black lettering. The first title will be 'Doom of an Axis Torpedo Factory.' . . ."

"Jesus F. Christ!" Dennis exploded.

Kane whirled on him, but Brockhurst was faster. Stepping between the two he blocked Kane with his shoulder.

"General Dennis, what's so tragic about destroying a torpedo factory? Aren't they worth-while targets?"

"The last one might be. The first twenty-odd will scarcely inconvenience them."

"But if it's a start . . . ?" persisted Brockhurst.

Dennis didn't care whether the correspondent ever learned the theory of bombardment or not but he had seen Kane and Garnett look at each other over that reminder. He amplified, speaking ostensibly to Brockhurst. "The navy can win the sub war in the Atlantic if they get their fingers out. Can they strike the Germans in Germany?"

Brockhurst nodded quietly but Garnett took it up now.

"You forget the interservice co-operation angle, Casey."

"Did you get my memorandum to your bosses on that?"

"He did not," said Kane. "You know that was too provocative."

"It was generous, sir," Dennis retorted. "I wrote them, Cliff, through channels, that I'd take any naval target in Germany the day after they took those battleships in and shelled the fighter plane factory at Bremen."

"Can I use that?" asked Brockhurst eagerly.

"God no!" said Kane. "Half the United Chiefs are admirals."

Kane had recognized that memorandum as one of the best staff papers he had ever seen, terse and undeniable with Dennis's clarity and force. He had pondered the possibility that it might cut through some of their overriding restrictions like a blowtorch. But he had had to ponder also the hazard of applying heat to higher councils.

"Sir," said Dennis, "may I send the order?"

"Casey, we *can't* lose another forty planes at Schweinhafen the day after we've told them we destroyed it."

"Sir, you can wait till the mission has taken off to send the correction. If you will release the Division to my discretion on the weather now . . ."

"No. Whichever of us got hung we'd still be sabotaging the Chief."

"If we don't we're sabotaging bombardment, sir."

2

Kane did not reply at once. He was conscious of the eyes upon him and acutely aware of the reservation with which Brockhurst was now palpably weighing everything he heard. But he was not thinking of Brockhurst or even of Dennis now. He would have to answer Dennis. What troubled him was answering the older questions which the Brigadier's passion had rekindled deep within Kane himself.

Frowning with abstraction he walked over to Dennis's desk, selected and cut a cigar through a silence so tense that Major Prescott did not even risk offering to light it for him. The steady drone of the motors outside carried clearly through the muffling of the blackout curtains; their insistence was a sound always in the background of his thought. It had reawakened another Kane.

"Casey," he said, "we're not *sure*. I've spent twenty-five years doing and preventing things that would have made or wrecked the Air Corps. The Chief has spent thirty. You don't realize how we've fought . . ."

"No?" challenged Martin.

"*No!*" Then, remembering where Martin had spent

the day, he softened his voice. "You're giving your youth. We've already given ours. Casey has named a son after Billy Mitchell . . . long after. We took Billy's side when it meant Siberia. They dead-ended the Chief in a cavalry school. I went with him and stayed. I amended the Army Regulation for the Disposal of Manure for him, in longhand. They didn't give us type-writers in those days.

"But we never gave up. We did those crazy publicity stunts and we kept our own fund for the widows. We wrote anything we could get printed, we went down on our knees to Hollywood for pictures, we tested without parachutes, we flew the mail through solid glue. The year Goering won the Munich Conference without throwing a bomb our whole appropriation wasn't as big as the New York City public safety budget . . . and we bought a lot of Congressmen liquor out of our own pockets to get it."

Memory quickened in him as he spoke. But now Brockhurst broke in.

"Why don't you tell this story?"

"You don't sell stories in uniform," said Kane. "We were still taking turns with obsolete junk when the country was told we were going to have an air force of fifty thousand planes. No one bothered to say how long it would take to make them, or how long it takes to make a pilot with a chance to live. Oh no! We were going to have fifty thousand planes and our boys were never going to fight in foreign wars. So the country went back to sleep and we started making a modern air force . . . out of promises . . . and what was left over after the best of our planes and teachers had been given to every goddamned ambassador in Washington."

"Wasn't that smart, to get experience?" asked Brock-hurst.

"There wasn't any experience for daylight precision bombardment. The Germans and British had tried it and said it couldn't be done. The Chief said it could. And there were times when some of us had to force his hand . . . but there was never a time when he wasn't taking the rap. We were just beginning to get the tools to get started when we were in it ourselves, with a double war and a fifty-thousand-plane paper air force that didn't add up to fifty serviceable bombers. . . ."

He shook his head, trying to clear it again. But when he looked up those steady gray eyes were still fixed inexorably upon him.

"Maybe we did boast and exaggerate. We had to get the public behind us. Who *was* telling the public the truth then? A hell of a lot of our stunting was encour-aged, higher up, to cover the difference between what the country was promised and what it had.

"We used to dream of Fortresses to use in mass for-mations of — *six!* My God, Casey, if we'd had, even in 1941, what you've lost this week we would have had a Munich of our own with the Japs that would have made Hitler's Munich look like a Rotary meeting. But instead we had diplomacy and a good-neighbor policy. Now we're beginning to get an Air Force and you want me to risk the whole thing on a premature showdown."

Losses hit Dennis below the belt. For him the hardest duty of the war had been learning to live with his losses. Night after night and hour after hour of every waking

158

day they were with him always in the background of everything he had done and the foreground of everything he must do.

He had thought about them as deeply as he could think without finding solace. What explanation there might be beyond the limitations of his own thought he did not know. He realized that he had spent the best efforts of an active mind on problems essentially rational, mechanical, and soluble. The freedom Dennis was entrusted to defend depended upon his killing Jenks. It must be done as an example to other young men who might be reluctant to kill or be killed in defense of the concept of freedom that biologically indistinguishable young men in Germany were similarly encouraged to destroy.

It had all been done before and would be done again. The battle cries differed; the end was homicide. Dennis judged, on past performance, that they would continue it, intermittently, until the race had achieved its only inferable purpose in extinction. The evidence seemed plain that of all the purposes men had, the most certain and recurrent was homicide.

The experiment of precision bombardment was, he still considered, a promising therapy. It could no more end wars than a doctor can confer immortality. It did appear to promise a quicker, cheaper termination of this particular homicidal fever than the previous practices of bloodletting by bayonet. It was unproved, but the idea of reducing opposition by disarmament rather than by death seemed sound, if feasible.

For this Dennis had taught himself to look past the doom in the strained young faces that swarmed off the trucks from the replacement centers. He himself had had a voice in determining the duration of the tour of duty that fixed the mathematical odds at two to one against the individual's survival. He had been able to do it by looking beyond the boys he could see toward the indeterminable point where this never-ending stream of immolation would finally stop. It was not enough to think of the boys who were here. He had to think of the ones who might be spared coming.

For this he knew that forty planes was cheap for a target of consequence. One boy killed for statistical effect was wanton murder. For this he knew that milk runs over France were a delusion that could only mean more telegrams to different families later. An occasional easy mission was, of course, indispensable. There had to be a limit to what was asked of any individual. The current requirement of twenty-five missions was as close to that limit as he had dared to recommend.

But, if the therapy was to succeed, the country had to get its bodies' worth out of those twenty-five missions. To send two hundred planes over an easy Channel target, even if they returned without a scratch, meant the loss, by graduation, of eight competent crews; it meant the country had to provide eight more green crews. It meant saving the boy who was here now to kill the boy who was training at home. By longer projection it meant saving aviators to kill infantrymen, in a ratio not determinable.

There were times when Dennis doubted that Kane remembered this. He knew that many of his senior's burdens were imponderables even more elusive than the terrible ratios which tormented himself. But some of these imponderables were part of a peacetime past. Kane was still fighting the bitter clinical disputes which had preceded this experiment in blood itself. It was possible that his long struggle for the knife had vitiated his capacity to use it.

Dennis had read that the human body replaces itself, tissue by tiny tissue, so systematically that every seven years sees a complete change in the structure. Studying Kane now he wondered if the human character and spirit likewise changed to different substance in the old mold under the same inexorable combustion of time and energy. This man fumbling with his apprehensions of past problems was not the Kane he had known. Or Dennis was not himself. Strain had changed one of them. To believe he was the one was to believe himself unfit for this command. It was possible but others had to judge that. Now he cut through the continuing tirade of Kane's lamentations curtly.

"Sir, that's all true. But the point of the whole struggle was to get the Air Force in time."

He walked over and tapped the Swastika on the wall.

"They're still ahead of us technically. It's enough. These things can be the end of bombardment unless we check them now."

"Casey," protested Kane, "I've lived with the things that can be the end of bombardment. Do you remember the fight to get our first Fort? Do you realize how the navy wants them now, for sub patrol and to protect the repairing of those battleships air power couldn't hurt? Do you realize how the Ground Forces want our pilots for company commanders? Do you know how the British want these Forts for night bombing? Do you know

161

there's a plan to fly infantry supplies to China *with bombers?* Do you know what the Russians want? Don't you realize the United Chiefs are half admirals, the Consolidated Chiefs half British? Don't you know why the whole Air Corps holds its breath every time the Prime Minister goes to Washington?

"On Tuesday every damned one of these factions will have a voice in that meeting. Every one has some pet reason for wanting us to fail, some sure-fire strategy of naval blockade or attrition by defensive, or building a road across the Himalayas, or breaking German morale with pamphlets or any other sure-fire way to keep a nice war going.

"Tuesday, this Tuesday, they'll be waiting for the Chief like buzzards and you want to send him in there with three days of prohibitive losses hanging over the allocation we need to prove our theory."

"Damn it, sir. It isn't a theory any more. We got Posenleben beyond fighters, with one division. And Ted did wreck that torpedo plant today even if it was the wrong target."

Martin held his breath at the outburst but this time it was with hope. Kane had his temper firmly in control again. He seemed to be measuring every word Dennis spoke. Rising now he walked over for a long look at the two red crosses before turning back to them. There was no trace of rancor in his gravity.

"I know, Casey. With time and planes we can do the same thing to any factory in Europe. But they *don't* know it yet and the whole thing's at stake here and now. It isn't just a matter of a few losses this week or even a lot in six months. The Germans are going to kill a lot more of our people. But they won't be any deader than all the ones who've been killed in the last thirty years, to give us air power.

"You can concentrate on Germany but I'm fighting the tough part of this war against the Ground Forces and the navy and the Congress and the White House and the people and the press and our goddamned allies, every one of them with a different idea of fighting this war just as the last one was fought, only more slowly.

"You think I don't know that the boys call me old Percent? You think I've enjoyed spreading this mug of mine around the press like a divorced heiress? You think I haven't known what they could do to me for the statistics I've juggled, the strike photos I've doctored, the reports I've gilded? You can worry about losses and you should. But I've spent twenty-five years watching men, my friends, killed and broken and disgraced and discarded for one single idea . . . to get us an Air Force. Now you want me to gamble the whole thing to save a few casualties next winter."

"Sir," said Dennis implacably, "if it were a few casualties we wouldn't be discussing it."

Kane relapsed into silence and Brockhurst felt a darkening presentiment. He knew that decisions like this one were not made on the abstract merits of the case. Dennis was sustaining the inequality of his position by sheer moral force because Kane was afraid of the moral force that sustained Dennis. But Brockhurst knew that men with power to do it destroy what they fear. Kane had the power.

And yet in this he was misjudging Kane as many men did. For Kane's mind, as always, was working far above

163

the levels of the present decision. He was acutely aware of that moral force in Dennis, aware of his own vacillation in the face of it. But he was thinking that what was troublesome at his level might be invaluable at another. If they had had a man of this determination in the last Congressional hearing, instead of that mealy-mouthed Lester whose brilliance never lost a point or won a fight . . .

Of course Dennis was young but Kane knew that this war would be the end of him and most of the old gang. They'd have to retire while their temporary ranks held. There wouldn't be another bonanza like this in their lives. Dennis would not retire. With one more star and a good war record a man like that could fight the navy. He had everything except caution.

Time was with Dennis and the young men now. They had the best war in history in their hands. If he could preserve Dennis, if he could fuse just enough caution into that power and passion . . .

The opening of the door broke his reverie. He looked up with a clearing snap of his head to see a young major hurrying in proudly with a weather map in his hand.

Chapter Ten

MAJOR DAVIS interrupted the conference with an unscientific sense of personal importance. He knew the impropriety of this feeling but could not resist it. For weary months he had been summoned and dismissed, like a bellhop. This time he bore information that warranted a voice in affairs. Haley had warned him that Kane himself was in the room. Davis had rejoiced in reminding Haley that there were no data indicating correlation between Kane's whereabouts and incipient Polar Turbulence. Dennis had told him to report change instantly. He had change to report. His confidence was confirmed, upon entrance, by the instant, complete attention he could always command from Dennis . . . for a minute.

"Excuse me, sir. You said if anything special . . ."

"Of course. Go right ahead, Major."

"We've a flash from Iceland, sir. Only preliminary but it does indicate a most interesting condition. A cold mass of a rather exceptional nature has formed eccentrically . . ."

"Never mind the genealogy," said Dennis. "What's it going to do?"

It was always like this. Davis compressed his indignation.

"Blanket the Continent, sir, if . . ."

"When?"

"On present indications late Monday afternoon unless . . ."

"When will it close my bases?"

"Best estimate now, sir, is any time after fifteen hundred Monday."

Davis held his tongue now. They could chew that one over and then ask him. But Dennis did not ask him. He burst out savagely.

"I always said God must love Willi Messerschmitt."

He brooded through a black silence and then, remembering Davis, nodded brief, absent-minded dismissal.

"Bring confirmations or further changes as they come in."

Davis retired with a frustrate and highly unscientific inner imprecation that the Army Air Forces and all their generals could go to hell.

Kane watched the closing of the door with an uneasiness he could only hope he was not showing. His mind had been made up even before he heard the weather. In the long run he knew that the Allies would win this war, jets or no jets. He had resolved to save Dennis for the permanent wars among the services. A man of his force was too valuable to be destroyed by misfortune in a temporary foreign campaign. He told himself now that the only question remaining was how to whip Dennis without breaking his spirit. Even to himself he did not yet admit a deeper uncertainty as to whether he could, in a showdown, whip Dennis at all. As if aware of this himself, the Brigadier was already challenging him again.

"There goes our summer, sir. We'll make it now or bite off our nails waiting for another chance."

"Casey, I'm sorry, but two more days of prohibitive losses just now . . ."

Dennis exploded.

"God damn it, sir, it's *not* a theory any longer. Can't you see why we're having these losses? Do you think the Germans would fight like this if they weren't scared of our bombardment?"

Martin saw Kane himself shake with this blast. But he checked himself and spoke to his aide.

"Homer, make a note of that, for the Chief."

Prescott whipped out a notebook, bent over the map table, and fixed his shocked eyes upon Dennis. The Brigadier, as if conscious of the narrowness of this momentary reprieve, paused for a minute before continuing with an earnest, low-voiced sincerity more moving than any vehemence.

"We've scarcely scratched Germany yet, sir, but look what we're doing to their Air Force. We're doing what no other weapon in this war has done or can do. We're making it fight, on *our initiative*, where it can't refuse in order to rest and rebuild. We are tearing it up *over Germany*. The German Air Force has been the balance of power in this whole war, ever since Munich. It took their Ground Forces everywhere they've been. It beat the Polish Air Force in three days, the Norwegian in three hours; it forced the Maginot Line and beat the French in three weeks . . ."

"Homer," said Kane, "be sure you're getting this."

"The Royal Air Force," continued Dennis, "won a brilliant battle from it but it was a defensive battle, over England. The German Air Force rested a little and then knocked off Yugoslavia and Greece for practice,

167

captured Crete, dominated the Mediterranean, chased the Russians to Moscow and the Volga, and got close enough to that Caspian oil to smell it. They blockaded the North Cape and very nearly cut the Atlantic life line to England itself. Peterson would have done it if Goering had given him two groups instead of one *Staffel*. And even after that they took Rommel to the gates of Alexandria.

"Now where is that German Air Force, sir? Already we've made them convert bomber groups to fighters, we've made them switch their whole production, procurement, and training programs. We've made them pull operational groups off the Russians and away from Rommel to put them over there, across the Channel, against us . . ."

He walked over and banged the map with his fist and his voice was rising again now.

"Now the Russians have been able to mount and sustain a counteroffensive. Our own people, in the Med, have air superiority and they're advancing with it . . ."

"Get every word of this, Homer," breathed Kane.

"Well, get this too, Homer," rasped Dennis. "The Germans know all of this better than we do. They've been willing to loosen their grip on their costliest conquests and break the whole balance of their Air Force for just one thing . . . to defend Germany itself from us. They've done it because they know something else. They know that fighters, Spits and Hurricanes, saved England from either decisive bombardment or invasion. Now they've got a better fighter than those were. They intend to make Europe as impregnable as the British made England. And they're going to do it, just as surely as we sit here with our fingers in our asses and let them!"

Prescott coughed discreetly through the enveloping silence.

"Do you want that in too, sir?"

Kane did not hear Prescott. He had been listening to Dennis. It was the burning sincerity of the plea which had illuminated again for him the old dream. He was seeing in fact the old vision of Air Power itself, the vision he had followed, the vision for which he and his kind had planned and pleaded and promised.

And yet it remained a glittering gamble. Kane knew far better than Dennis how bitterly the levels above him were torn with their own disunities, political, strategic, nationalistic, now that they had achieved the suppression of air power to an auxiliary level. He knew the quarrels and compromises, the delays and disagreements, the wary stalemates between military strategy and international policy, the sacrifices of lives to save faces and of faces to save the fears that were older than any passing war.

Kane looked past the waiting Dennis to the map now, but even as his quickening eyes swept toward Germany they hung on the chalk marks on the loss column of the Ops board. He shook his head heavily and clearly heard Prescott repeat his frightened question.

"No, not that part exactly, Major. Just the sense of it. Casey, I agree with you entirely, my boy, but we've simply got to wait till we're a little stronger."

"Sir," said Dennis, and they could all see him controlling himself with evident effort now, "wars are lost by waiting. If it were a question of potential strength there wouldn't be any wars. It isn't like that. Decisions are won

169

by the margins available at critical times and places. The Allies waited, at Munich. The French and British waited, behind the Maginot Line. The Germans waited, for a little more relative strength to invade England. The Russians waited, until they had to take on the German armies without an ally in the field. We waited, for more strength to coerce Japan.

"Now we're forcing the fighting, at terrible disadvantages of distance, defenses, and weather . . . on a margin so thin we cross ourselves before counting losses . . . with a bomber that thirty-millimeter cannon will make obsolete. But we're doing it. We have, *now*, the advantage of the offensive, precariously, but we've got it. Advantage is cumulative. If we stop now and wait for the cycle to swing again we'll be waiting for them to put a roof on the Continent. I'm not trying to tell you that Operation Stitch will win the war. But no battle anywhere in this war has been won without aerial supremacy. Operation Stitch is the price of that."

He stopped. The muffled drumming of the motors outside and the clacking of the teleprinter in the Ops room filled part of the silence; the rest of it hung heavily over them all. Kane knew now that Dennis was not going to yield. He could relieve him, of course. But Dennis believed these things and would say them elsewhere, anywhere, even in Washington itself if Kane sent him back there. On the other hand, if Washington itself decided to relieve him . . . Kane shook his head and rose with quick decision, the others springing up after him.

"Will you gentlemen wait in the anteroom, please."

He saw Garnett's angry flush at being included with

the other ranks but he offered no modification of the order. After a second Garnett followed the others out, closing the door himself.

"Casey, I'm taking Cliff back to my headquarters with me at once and releasing the Division to your discretion."

"Thank you, sir," said Dennis quietly.

Kane hesitated, wishing to say more, remembering that the spoken word cannot be unsaid. Dennis did not need things spelled out for him, but his own deep, haunting anxiety made Kane speak against his wiser instincts.

"Casey, you realize what can happen?"

"Perfectly, sir."

"Well, I hope it doesn't. Good luck, my boy."

He was turning toward the door when Evans stepped in from the Ops room, reluctantly extending a sheet of teleprint paper.

"Top Secret relay from General Kane's headquarters for the General, sir."

2

After observing Dennis's defense of Goldberg that evening Sergeant Evans had gone to the Top Secret Files and read the plan labeled Operation Stitch. One perusal of it confounded him. The army, or at least the Fifth Division, did have a sensible, logical plan. Evans was dazed until he remembered what was going on in the next room. That confirmed it all. This plan was so good that it was requiring the exertions of a major general to resist its use.

Evans had shaken his head, wondering why Dennis had not already been court-martialed. And yet Kane was evidently vacillating. Against all previous experience, Evans himself had begun to hope when the reality of the clattering teleprinter spelled out the message he now handed General Kane.

Standing by at attention he watched Kane wilt visibly through a quick reading of it before handing on the message to Dennis.

"It's from Les Blackmer, Casey."

Dennis read aloud slowly: "Impossible contact Chief yet. Considered opinion here implores moderation and low losses during critical three days next especially in view of Part Two which follows. Two; you are again advised imminent visit three high-ranking members House of Representatives Military Affairs Committee, arriving Prestwick probably this night. Contact Embassy at once. Representative Malcolm will particularly wish to see his nephew, Captain Lucius Malcolm Jenks O–886924371 your command. Suggest his assignment special escort duty this visit and must remind how opportune would be decoration Captain Jenks if eligible either presently or prospectively end Washington signal Casey for God's sake find General Kane and tell him wise men from west already Prestwick arriving Croydon daylight Embassy frantic signed Saybold for Kane."

Dennis lowered the paper slowly. But Kane did not wait to hear.

"Sorry, Casey. You will put maximum sorties and tonnage on the safest naval target you can find, under fighter cover, tomorrow. I'll take Jenks with me in my car and make . . . er . . . medical arrangement."

"Sir, this is impossible."

"Nothing's impossible, Casey. We're doing it."

172

Dennis wheeled on Evans. "Sergeant, get those two officers . . ."

Evans sprang for the door. Kane did not speak until it had closed. His voice was regretful but firm.

"The charges will be quashed. We'll have a formal presentation for the visiting fireman here tomorrow, timed so they can lunch afterward and then watch the return of the mission. You will instruct any plane sufficiently damaged to jeopardize landing to use one of the other stations. I'll have a citation written for Jenks in my office tonight. . . ."

He looked up indignantly as the door opened and two officers wearing medical insignia appeared. Their faces were puffy and their blouses ruffled from sleep but the elder saluted smartly.

"Dayhuff and Getchell reporting as ordered, sir."

"General Kane," said Dennis. "Major Dayhuff is my Division Medical Officer. Captain Getchell is flight surgeon of Jenks's group."

"Well . . ." Kane did not extend his hand.

"Major, tell General Kane exactly what you told me."

"General Kane, there is no satisfactory medical explanation of Captain Jenks's conduct. He acknowledges this and says he expects no medical exoneration."

Thoroughly alert now, Kane studied the doctors closely. A presentiment was warning him to caution, as it had warned him earlier in the evening, against a showdown with Dennis. He spoke more civilly, feeling his way.

"Mightn't that in itself be an indication of neurosis?"

"Doctors can be wrong, sir. In our opinion he's normal."

173

"Have you made a formal record of this?"

"Not yet, sir. We shall."

"Do you think this is simple fear . . . cowardice, Major?"

"No, sir. Any man in his right mind is afraid to fly these missions. The cowards welcome a medical excuse not to. This man apparently doesn't want one."

"Have you any idea of why he refused to fly?"

Dayhuff nodded a graying head to his junior. Captain Getchell chose his words with slow, conscientious care.

"We don't consider this a medical matter, sir. But Captain Jenks has mentioned some of his ambitions to me, in fact to anyone who would listen. He has been very frank to say that he intends to make something out of this war."

"How?"

"Politically, I believe, sir. At first Jenks made a noticeable effort to be popular in the Group but the effect was . . . well, contrary to his hopes. His operational training phase was not harmonious. By the time we entered combat status he was distrusted by the others and very resentful. When the men rode him he used to say that not only they but the whole army would come begging to his door someday and then they'd learn something about who ran the country."

"Mightn't that, in itself, indicate . . . er . . . instability?"

"Sir," said Dayhuff, "if we took to diagnosing ambition for an aberration we'd be busier than we are."

"Thank you very much, gentlemen," said Kane.

They saluted and withdrew. As they went Dennis noted that Evans had re-entered with them and over-

174

heard the conversation. He dismissed the Sergeant with an abrupt nod of his head.

"Casey," asked Kane thoughtfully, "are these doctors our own?"

"No, sir. Civilian reservists."

"Hmmm. Of course we can get Jenks to our own people . . ."

"One of these men is from Mayo and the other from Hopkins, sir. They will sign the report."

Dennis had hoped that he would not have to do this. He knew now that he would and he was a little surprised at the calmness that possessed him.

It had been like this when he was testing. All through the preparation there were doubt and nervousness and tension. Then, with the take-off, those things dropped behind. It became very simple. A man did all he could first to eliminate needless risk. Then he forced the intended risk until something broke . . . sometimes the plane, sometimes the man, sometimes the prevailing boundaries of gravity and momentum. Dennis had done it before; he was going to do it again now. He studied Kane's troubled irresolution as calmly as he had once studied his instruments before nosing down.

"Umm. We've got to do *something*, Casey."

"I know a way, sir."

"What?"

"If Jenks had been acting under direct, secret orders to hold himself in readiness for this escort duty and to discontinue flying missions until he had performed it, he would have been justified in refusing the mission without explanation. If the right orders, suitably dated, had been delayed, in channels, in this headquarters . . ."

175

Kane got it at once.

"Exactly, Casey, exactly. I won't forget this, my boy."

"I'll attend to the whole thing," said Dennis, "*as soon as I've ordered the Schweinhafen mission for tomorrow.*"

He saw Kane's face twitch.

"Casey, this sounds like blackmail."

"You've told me, sir, that there were times when you forced the Chief's hand."

Kane managed a smile now. "You have your orders."

Dennis looked deliberately at his watch. "Then at five-nineteen I charge Jenks with desertion in the face of the enemy."

"General, I order you to release Captain Jenks to me."

"I understand the order, sir. But the charges will be filed, the evidence heard, and the trial held in this headquarters unless you promise me Schweinhafen tomorrow and Fendelhorst the next day I judge suitable."

"Casey, really, my boy, this is preposterous. If you'll just consider . . ."

"I have considered, sir."

"You realize that I might not be able to . . . protect you?"

"I do, sir."

"Well, if you want to take the personal risk I *can* release the Division. . . . I was really going to anyway before that signal. . . ."

Dennis had already picked up the black Admin phone. He kept his back on Kane while ordering Jenks's release to the Major General's personal custody, so as to give Kane time to collect himself. When Dennis faced him again Kane managed an air of sorrowful gravity.

"In the circumstances, Casey, I'll have to signal Washington the correction on today's strike."

"I understand that, sir."

"Well, don't come to the gate."

With an angry slam of the door Kane was gone. Turning in his tracks Dennis opened the Ops door and shouted for Haley. His face was calm when the startled Colonel appeared.

"Put Stitch, phase two, Schweinhafen, on the printer at once for all groups for tomorrow. Bomb and fuel loadings as before; routes and timings to follow. . . ."

Martin hurried in from the anteroom now.

"Casey, Percent went out of here burning like a fuse. What the hell did you do?"

"Twisted his tail a little. Get going, Haley."

"Sir, you're sure you mean Schweinhafen?"

"Certain. I'll sign it in a minute but get it clicking."

Haley raised appealing eyes to inform the heavens that this was none of his work and hurried out the door.

3

The door had hardly closed on Haley before Martin's anxiety expressed itself.

"Quit smirking and tell me what you did."

"I traded him Jenks for Schweinhafen and Fendelhorst. Jenks's uncle Malcolm of the House Military Affairs Committee arrives here tomorrow."

"Casey, this is suicide. Percent can phone Washington."

"Well, it was the last card. He might play straight."

"Might."

"You can't tell, Ted. I can remember when Kane had guts. Let's go to work."

He had started for the Ops room door when Martin's voice stopped him.

"Casey, Cliff said Helen wants me to pick a godfather for the kid. Will you take it?"

He was so pleased that he had to hesitate a second to cover his embarrassment.

"You trying to queer it for life?"

"I'm serious, Casey."

"Well, sure."

"And I want you to promise me something."

"What?"

"If he ever wants to join the goddamned army you'll take a club and beat his brains right out through his tail."

"I know what you mean," said Dennis slowly.

Martin walked over to him now, unpinning the wings from his blouse as he came.

"But after you get 'em beaten out he'll probably become a pilot. If he does, give him these."

He extended the wings. Dennis looked from them to Martin's face without moving a hand.

"Nuts. All I owe him's a silver cup and a blameless example through life. You give him those yourself."

"You keep 'em, I might lose 'em."

"No you don't, Ted. You're sitting here, biting your fingernails, tomorrow."

Martin shook his head. "No dice, Casey. Schweinhafen's mine."

Dennis had known this was coming and had meant to prepare himself for final, unequivocal decision but there had not been time. There never was time. He looked at the set face before him and tried to stall until his head cleared.

"Listen, Ted. Any of the others can . . ."

"Not tomorrow. They hear too well."

He knew his own face must be twitching now as Kane's had.

"What do you mean?"

"You know damned well what I mean. Percent can double-cross you with a counterorder from Washington and signal a recall or change of target after we've started."

"I . . . I had thought of that but . . ."

"You won't have to tomorrow. Let's go. I'll get some benzedrine and meet you in the Ops room."

Dennis felt the impact of metal in his palm and tried to speak but no sound followed Martin.

Chapter Eleven

ELMER BROCKHURST had thought that in the course of the war he had attended enough staff, command, and press presentations to inure his stomach to anything he might hear. But on the bright Sunday morning of the second Schweinhafen mission he sat in General Dennis's office, listening to the presentation General Kane was staging for the visiting Congressmen with a feeling of degradation that occasionally bordered upon nausea.

For this ceremony the office had been transformed into a miniature theater. Brockhurst himself, the three Congressmen, Prescott, Garnett, and Dennis were the audience, seated in a little semicircle facing Kane, who lectured them, using for illustration a series of wallboard-mounted exhibits which Evans held up in turn upon the map table.

Through the open windows came the intermittent droning of the motors in the repair hangars but it was only a feeble, fitful chorus. The parking stands were bare again. The faint whine from the stratosphere was a solitary ice-cream sortie, timed to brighten the impending lunch party.

". . . and now, gentlemen," Kane continued blandly, "because Naval Objectives are such a vital part of our overall strategy I have had Major Prescott prepare for you a special presentation on 'The Doom of an Axis Torpedo Factory.'"

Prescott stepped briskly to the center of the stage, took the pointer from Kane, and raised a folder in his hand so that the audience could plainly see the oversized TOP SECRET lettering upon the cover. Kane seated himself and accepted a cigarette from Congressman Malcolm. Prescott waited through the lighting of it before beginning solemnly.

"I am compelled by duty, gentlemen, to remind you that the contents of this Directive, which General Kane has authorized me to read you, are . . . TOP SECRET."

He paused with the insinuating hesitancy of a strip teaser fingering the first buttons. Brockhurst saw the Congressmen stir and quicken in their seats. He noticed also a faint, rippling readjustment of the jaw muscles which had locked Dennis's face into the bleak, expressionless mask he knew so well.

It was only, Brockhurst knew, in the details of its staged prevarication that this particular presentation differed from others he had heard. As far as he knew the Presentation was one of the many military novelties of this war. The device had had a reasonable origin. The theory had been, in the beginning, that these functions informed the commander.

Since no man could keep the details of ever-changing global warfare in his head no man tried to. They were kept in the heads and files of batteries of staff officers. These men read the news, the signals from other commands, the discoveries of Intelligence, the reports from lower echelons, and even the public prints. These, in continuous process, they digested, compared, and collated, changing colored pins on maps and lines on graphs with indefatigable intent to simplify. Then at the appointed time daily the great man, of whatever command, seated himself and absorbed this predigested knowledge as painlessly as possible from the voices, maps, charts, diagrams, statistics, and, finally, the opinions of his underlings.

From its humble beginning the institution of the War Room Presentation had grown. The drama inherent in the daily ceremony could not resist improving upon itself. War rooms became the showcases of Command, the artful illustrations of alibi.

Presentations were coached until they became fullfledged daily theatricals to which commanders led important guests with serene confidence of the desired impression. For as information became drama its reporters kept pace with tacit understanding that the actor's first duty is to please. From the brutality of the ancient tradition that the bearer of bad news is beheaded, the War Room Presentation had advanced so far that bad news simply was not borne.

And over it all the dark, dramatic mantle of military secrecy spread its protective folds.

". . . we knew, gentlemen," Major Prescott continued, "that this one factory was manufacturing sixty-one point three per cent of the delicate timing mechanism for warheads . . ."

Had anyone been looking, Brockhurst's expression might have seemed cynical.

". . . and so, gentlemen" — Major Prescott dropped his voice an octave and the Congressmen obediently leaned forward — "we attacked. On this panel you see the pictures of the factory *before* . . ."

Brockhurst watched Evans shift the panels without expression and wondered what the Sergeant was thinking. Evans was thinking of his conversation with the warrant officer, a leathery old cavalry man, who had delivered the thirty-odd chunks of wallboard in a special truck from General Kane's headquarters that morning before dawn.

"No war room?" asked the warrant officer. "'What the hell does General Dennis do?"

"Plans missions," said Evans. "Ever heard of them?"

Together they had remodeled Dennis's office for the purpose. Major Prescott had appeared presently, sleepless but fresh with excitement. It had been his idea to dispense with the expert scene shifters in favor of Evans. He had pointed out to Kane that a certain mechanical crudeness would probably be even more effective than their usual polished performance.

Prescott and the warrant officer had coached Evans to their satisfaction before Prescott retired to study his lines. Evans had decided that he could afford some of the combat crews' fresh eggs in exchange for further confidences. Under their influence the warrant officer had thawed for commiseration.

"Better hit the latrine first," he concluded.

"It's as bad as that?"

"Prescott won't bother you unless you got a weak stummick," said the warrant officer, "but that Kane he could put his mouth to a horse's ass and blow the bridle off its head."

2

Dennis became aware that Major Prescott had finished. He judged it was five minutes since he had looked at his wrist watch and decided it was absurd to stick to his resolution not to look at it again for ten. The glance showed him it had been two and a half.

By now Ted was well beyond fighter cover but yesterday they had had thirty-four minutes before the shooting began. Even allowing that they had not picked up the expected tail wind east of Paris . . . He shook his head and made a new resolution to concentrate on Kane, who was about to resume the major part of the presentation. The signal would come when it came. Nothing he might think now would alter it.

As Prescott resumed his seat the glowing glances of the Congressmen showed Dennis why Kane kept him for an aide. He could see that even Garnett was impressed with what the Major had made out of yesterday's mission. With an inner chuckle he wondered suddenly how long Kane would be able to keep Prescott. Garnett was just the man to arrange wider horizons for an aide who could snatch triumph out of disaster as fluently as Prescott. Then his chuckle sobered on the reflection that Garnett himself might not now be returning to wider horizons.

"Finally, gentlemen," said Kane, "we come to the health of our personnel. If there is one thing a commander must be vigilant about it is the physical and moral welfare of his troops. We never forget that the nation has given us these boys in trust. Graph, Sergeant."

Evans held up another chunk of wallboard, crisscrossed with multicolored graph lines.

"I have issued a directive throughout our command," continued Kane, "that the orders of doctors are final authority. Sometimes it has ironic results. One of our officers knew he was overdue for the dentist recently but like most men he tried to put it off. However, when the inspecting lieutenant said: 'Sir, I must remind you of the Commanding General's directive . . .' Well, gentlemen, I went to the dentist."

He grimaced ruefully and waited. There was a second of hesitation before Prescott cued with a laugh which enabled the Congressmen to get the point. Brockhurst watched the trio from America react. Field and Stone smiled dutifully now but the whole room resounded to the booming tumult of Malcolm's belated laughter.

"Good God! Ain't that rich? . . . Majuh Gennel bein' sent to the dentis' by a damn *loo*tenan' . . . I declah! You ain't fixin' to do us like that, are you, Gennel?"

Something in the riotous volatility of that laughter reminded Brockhurst of Huey Long. Malcolm looked plumper on the surface but there was power in that heavy figure, and shrewdness in the little eyes. Malcolm had invaded this drab little island in the full protective coloration of his native jungle. He wore a lavender shirt with matching tie, a diamond stickpin, and bright yellow

185

shoes. The white felt hat now rested halfway back on his bald skull in acknowledgment of his presence indoors. In these somber surroundings he looked like a prosperous clown. His native state was strewn with the political corpses of men who had thought him one.

"Unfortunately, Mr. Malcolm," said Kane, "my Directive gives me no jurisdiction over the health of the Congress."

He let Malcolm laugh again before sobering briskly to work.

"This, gentleman, is our command's overall health record compared with twenty years' peacetime averages for the whole army."

His pointer traced the rise and fall of the curves rapidly.

"You will note that in almost every instance our curves of incidence are substantially below normal. This is respiratory complaint, this curve digestive, this one neurosis, a point of particular pride for our rest house and morale program. The American boy, gentlemen, is a very healthy young animal."

He paused with the patient innocence of art concealing its art, and Brockhurst watched Mr. Field reach naïvely for the bait.

"What's that red curve that sticks up so high, General?"

"The history of war, gentlemen, has always shown a remarkable affinity between Mars and Venus. I have observed that the American boy is a healthy animal and that condition produces its own paradox. The red curve is our rate of venereal disease."

"Mahs an' Venus!" roared Malcolm. "Good God ain't

186

that rich! Looks to me like one thing heahabout ain't rationed noway."

"Well, of course, gentlemen" — Kane feigned an exaggerated gravity — "that's the one argument that could be produced for our switching to *military* bombardment at night." He let them smile over this and then continued briskly again. "You can see that our curve is going back down to normal now."

Obligingly, Mr. Field reached again. "What put it up for that period, may I ask, General?"

"A factor over which a simple soldier has no control, sir — springtime."

This time it was Mr. Stone who broke the silence that followed Malcolm's laughter again. Stone, Brockhurst had noticed, was the most attentive of the three, a bleak, graying man of fifty whose taciturnity had prepared Brockhurst for his New England twang. It sounded rueful now.

"Well, happens so in our paaat of the world, too."

Kane beat Malcolm to it this time with a booming laugh of his own. Dennis's watch now showed him that there were six minutes more he would never have to live again.

"That, gentlemen," said Kane, "is a little résumé of this command's part in the big effort. I am at your service."

Malcolm bounced from his seat as if sprung. Then, with the floor won, he hesitated, head down, hands deep in his pockets, round face grave with solemnity now.

"Gennel, we are deeply grateful. I think I can speak foh my colleagues an' foh ouah country in thankin' you fum the bottom of ouah heahts. It ain't a easy matteh to

187

express the things a man feels to come oveh heah onto foreign soil an' find the American flag flyin' an' undeh it a fiel' commandeh who is woythy, not only of the great nation that sent him heah, but of the American boys he comman's. When we get back to ouah own post of duty in the Congress of the people in Washin'ton, an' I can see ouah civilian leadehs theah, most of whom I am fohtunate enough to count among my closes' frien's, I can promise you theah goin' to know fum my own lips how fohtunate this country is in some of its gennels."

Kane did not bat an eye.

"Thank you, Mr. Malcolm. You will do the country a greater service if you can make the people at home realize that the full credit belongs to our boys. I have always thought of command as a trusteeship, bestowed by the people who send us these boys, upon us who have to take them and train them and guide them and protect them until we finally face the awful decision of sending them into battle.

"War gives commanders little time for religious thought, gentlemen, but in our darkest hours I find comfort in the teachings of our chapel at West Point. Often at night I think back on the parable of the talents. There must have been moments of terrible discouragement for those servants who were trying to serve their Master as best they could with what was given them.

"There is a great lesson for all of us in their fidelity, but I think the greater lesson is to be found in the humility those experiences teach us about the wisdom of the Master who knew what he was doing when he tested his subordinates. Sometimes I have had to pray that our shortages and inadequacies here are only a test through

188

which the Greater Wisdom is measuring our faith and
confidence in the people we serve. . . ."

He let his voice trail off into a subdued silence, wondering, as always, whether he had overdone it. Ordinarily he would not have worked so hard on any delegation
below the Senate level. Prescott had said that the touch
of the parable put this effort into the Cabinet caliber.
But this was not an ordinary situation.

The accident of Malcolm's relation to Jenks had delivered this trio into Kane's hands before even the Hemisphere Commander had a chance to harden their ears.
It was not an opportunity to miss.

Of Malcolm, Kane was serenely confident. The Jenks
affair was a sword of many blades, as Dennis had taught
him. Stone was a cold fish; he had the look of a man who
remembered his regional folklore of wooden nutmegs.
Kane was still worrying about him when the innocuous-
looking Mr. Field cut through the echoes of his sermon
with a pointed question.

"You mean you want more planes, General?"

3

Dismayed as he was Kane showed no trace of
his inner misgiving. Field had been docile enough
through the military matters, following every statistic
with the quiet attentiveness of the earnest Pilgrim. The
case hung on getting him back to figures. Inwardly cursing the impulse that had made him risk oratory on Congressmen, Kane reverted to crisp bluntness.

"If the nation wants aerial supremacy we must have
them, sir."

Field looked thoughtfully at the map and scratched the back of his head. Stone spoke up now with troubled sincerity.

"The nation wants aerial supremacy everywhere, General. They all tell us the same thing; the people from India, China, Africa, Australia, the navy, the British, the Russians . . ."

"I'm sure they have their problems, Mr. Stone. But a simple field commander would be overreaching his duty to try to evaluate the higher strategy. I only know that my boys have been given the most important and difficult mission of this war."

"How do you figure that, General?" Field's question was mild enough but Kane did not need a second lesson in the penetration behind that mildness. It was touch and go but he had worked hard, through the night, and he was confident of his memory. He paused, frowning as if summoning words of his own.

"Because it is our mission, sir, to destroy the German Air Force. We are doing what no other weapon in this war has done or can do. We're making it fight, *on our initiative*, over Germany where it can't refuse. We are tearing it up *over Germany*. The German Air Force has been the balance of power in this war ever since Munich. . . ."

Brockhurst, recognizing the rhythm of these words now, glanced at Dennis. The Brigadier was studying the sky outside the window intently. Brockhurst saw him raise his left arm as if to look at his wrist watch but instead of doing so he lowered it into his lap again and kept his eyes fixed in the sky.

Turning, Brockhurst saw Prescott checking off sen-

190

tence after sentence as Kane continued through the speech. Kane had a bad minute or two with the sequence of the campaigns but he got through them. Then, as if sensing the relief in Prescott's face, he swept on with gathering confidence. The Congressmen were entirely his now. They were leaning forward with rapt concentration as Kane came to a carefully amended conclusion of the speech.

". . . we are pinning that Air Force down in Germany, gentlemen, destroying its factories by systematic plan and destroying its effective, operational planes by combat. We are winning aerial supremacy and the reinforcements you give us are the price of that supremacy."

Brockhurst stole another glance at Dennis and there stirred in the back of his mind some lines he had not recalled for years:

> If you can bear to hear the truth you've spoken
> Twisted by knaves to make a trap for fools, . . .

But Dennis was not hearing it. Brockhurst doubted that he was even aware of it. His eyes were still on the sky outside. The only sign he showed of having heard Kane's conclusion was to glance briefly at his wrist watch.

"Gennel," said Malcolm. "I consideh that a mastehful summary, mastehful."

"Thank you, Mr. Malcolm. I hope I've been able to show you . . ."

"General," said Stone, "that's interesting but we have other problems, too. The air war isn't the only one."

"We never forget that, Mr. Stone. We hold it a high

privilege to pave the way for our companion services. No battle in this war has been won without aerial supremacy, as I pointed out."

"That may be true here," said Field. "But the navy thinks . . ."

"Sir, co-operation with naval objectives is one of our foremost commitments. You gentlemen have just heard Major Prescott explain how General Dennis sent this division all the way to Gritzenheim to knock out the most significant torpedo factory in Europe. We knew it would cost us heavy losses but if there's one thing this command prides itself on it's looking at the war as a whole. Ample replacements are essential if we're to continue fulfilling that part of our directive which gives naval objectives a very high priority among our target categories."

"You're getting most of the available replacements now," said Stone. "What did you say your loss rate is?"

"Loss and claim chart again, Sergeant."

Evans shuffled through the exhibits and produced another twenty square feet of wallboard. Its essential information, like that of the rest, could have been written clearly on a playing card.

"Overall rate four point nine per cent so far, sir."

"That's computed up to . . . ?" Field persisted patiently.

"Last Sunday, sir," said Kane quickly. "We only total calculations at the end of each week."

"What are losses this week, General?"

"I'll have to tell you tomorrow, Mr. Stone, when I've heard from all the divisions."

He nodded quickly to Evans for removal of the board

but Malcolm spoke up now with authority in his slow accents.

"Just a minute, Sahgent, till I see if I can get this thu my haid. What were losses in this division, Gennel?"

Kane hesitated. "Have you the figures, General Dennis?"

Dennis rose before answering. "Ninety-four lost outright, five in the Channel, and thirty-odd damaged beyond economical repair, sir."

Brockhurst saw both Kane and Garnett start at the mention of the planes in the Channel and the Category E's. These were never included in public reports. The explanation was that such information might comfort an enemy who presumably did not know of them, after several years of his own cross-Channel bombing operations. Malcolm appeared to cogitate before proceeding with silky deliberation.

"Neah about a hund'ed an' thirty, out of what overall strength, Gennel Dennis?"

"It varies with the replacement flow, sir. The average runs from one eighty to two hundred."

Malcolm's face clouded over slowly as if with pain.

"That would mean betteh than sixty puh cent in this division against youah overall average of less than five, wouldn't it, Gennel Kane?"

"For this division, for this week, yes," admitted Kane. "But we had two exceptionally bad days. When these losses are figured into the aggregate average . . ."

"I undehstan' the aggregate average, suh, but I don't undehstan' this discrepancy between Gennel Dennis's division an' the othehs. Perhaps Gennel Dennis will explain his own self."

Dennis spoke with quiet patience: "This division has the only extension tanks for especially distant targets, sir. Both these operations were beyond the range of friendly fighter escort."

"An' the boys who were lost were deliberately sent beyon' the range of friendly fighteh coveh?"

"Yes."

"May I ask who ohdehed these operations?"

"I did."

"On youah own authority?"

"Yes."

Kane intervened quickly now, showing obvious agitation.

"General Dennis was quite within his authority, Mr. Malcolm. It happened that when these particular attacks were ordered I was too engrossed with other duties to keep myself entirely cognizant of the changing weather picture. In those circumstances all divisions are released to commanders' discretion."

"I undehstan' the technicalities, Gennel Kane. No one expec's a man of youah responsibilities to plan every attack foh every division every night." He paused to let the exoneration sink in before continuing. "But the fac's appeah to be that the minute youah back was turned Gennel Dennis took it on his own self to ohdeh these disastrous attacks . . ."

"They were not disastrous," said Dennis evenly. "Posenleben was the best piece of bombing in this war. As for yesterday . . ."

"That was a great success," interrupted Kane. "The navy has been very eager for us to destroy that torpedo plant. It was a great piece of interservice co-operation and a very bright spot in General Dennis's record."

Brockhurst had heard and read and indeed written too many official lies to be troubled about this one. What troubled him now was that he did not understand how Dennis had forced Kane to permit the second attack on Schweinhafen. Methods were usually visible through men; in this case they should have been transparent. Kane would respond, in extremity, only to fear. What had Dennis been able to make him fear?

Brockhurst had had a glimpse, indeed a clinical scrutiny, of the things Kane feared in the conference last night. There were coils within coils of the man's mainspring but they added up to ambition. Whether it was for himself or for the Air Forces was immaterial; the years had made them one. They had also made him as prudent as a turtle. Now he was permitting desperate risks for stakes so high and at a cost so sickening as to jeopardize the whole service.

Brockhurst knew that he had lost his news story already. The Air Forces would never dare to release the news of jets until the climax forced it out in alibi or exultation. It was a pattern bitterly familiar. The battleship men had denied bombs until they had to fight a naval war for landing fields; the tankers had explained away the 88-millimeter gun to the satisfaction of everyone but the crews who fought it. The story would be ended before it could be told.

And yet in this variation of the old pattern Brockhurst scented a new ending, perhaps the beginning of a new

195

pattern, attainable by immediate, courageous counter-measure, by Stitch in time. Against the whole tradition of the uniform Dennis was forcing it on a superior. How?

Brockhurst would never learn from Kane. The Major General had rejoined them in the anteroom last night smoldering with a chagrin he could not conceal, a fear more powerful than his fear of the press. He had told Brockhurst bluntly that he was summoned to London on secret military business. Only under blunt duress had his prudence reawakened to compromise; he would meet Brockhurst at the Division Headquarters next morning and redeem his promise of the full story later.

Brockhurst had spent a wakeful night in a neighboring pub until the roar of the departing bombers confirmed his surmise. Dennis had won. How?

An unfortunate mishap had delayed the correspondent's return to the Headquarters. He had left his car in the street outside the village pub. During the night some rascals had picked the lock cleanly and made off with a case of whiskey.

Brockhurst drank little himself. He and *Coverage* both considered that whiskey comes by its fullest value in other men's mouths. But the loss of a case in the island's drought was serious. He had complained to the pub-keeper, who replied indignantly that it was impossible; all Americans had been confined to their bases during the night. The man's indignation took on heat from a private conjecture that one of his own neighbors must have excluded him from such a wizard do. It was the war; it corrupted everyone.

Brockhurst had reached Headquarters just as the Congressmen were settling to Kane's presentation. He instantly recognized their presence as part of the puzzle but Kane used it cunningly to shield himself from further questioning. The correspondent could not tell yet whether Kane was defending Dennis or adroitly cutting his throat.

"Gennel Kane," said Malcolm, "I honoh youah loyalty to youah subohdinate commandeh, but it looks to me like ouah boys are payin' a pretty bloody price foh Gennel Dennis's recohd."

"They're paying a bloody price for the whole country's record, Mr. Malcolm," said Dennis quietly.

"You consideh the country's responsible foh you sendin' these boys beyon' frien'ly fighteh coveh?"

"Yes."

"How?"

"How did you vote on the fortification of Guam?"

"*What?*"

"How did you vote on the fortification of Guam?"

Stone's chuckle broke a perceptible silence.

"By God, Aaaathur, he's got you."

Malcolm's ruddy face was turning livid.

"We'll see who's got who . . ."

"Arthur," said Field evenly, "it's not our place to criticize operations. What are you attacking today, General Kane?"

"Why . . . as you gentlemen know, I was on my way to you at the time of the determinative weather conference. I think General Dennis can explain the details more clearly than I."

As if unconscious of Malcolm now, Dennis walked

quietly to the wall, stripped the masking curtain from the map, and pointed with a finger as he explained unemotionally.

"This is a three-pronged operation today, gentlemen. General Salmond's division is attacking the Brest shipyards and sub pen. General Endicott's division will attack a submarine repair yard at Emden almost simultaneously. The Fifth Division is attacking the Focke-Schmidt aircraft factory at Schweinhafen."

The others crowded to the map for a closer examination. Brockhurst noticed that General Kane's red cross through Schweinhafen had been erased during the night. The black markings indicating Schweinhafen and Fendelhorst gained prominence from the proximity of the heavy red cancellation of Posenleben. Malcolm scowled at them thoughtfully.

"Seems to me I heard this division attacked Schweinhafen yestehday, Gennel."

"The target was cloud-covered, Mr. Malcolm," said Kane quickly, "Colonel Martin, who had been instructed for that very contingency, very wisely decided to take the torpedo factory instead, knowing how long we had been planning on it. It was a wonderful piece of air generalship, gentlemen. Colonel Martin is our outstanding flying commander."

Stone pondered: "Is that the Martin who was in hot water over plane tests a few years ago?"

Kane smiled benignly. "Colonel Martin was a very impetuous young man, Mr. Stone, but those qualities are standing us in good stead now."

Field nodded now with an air of remembrance. "It seems to me, if I recollect rightly, that plane he com-

198

plained of never did come to much. Will we have a chance to meet him?"

"Later," said Dennis. "He's leading the Division today."

Dennis had stood alone on the roof of a Group Ops tower to watch the take-off. Heavy ground mist had blanketed the lowlands during the night. It clung still like a three-dimensional blotter over everything. For brief seconds he had been alone in the damp grayness with a troubled broken silence that swirled and eddied around him like the fingers of the mist itself.

Every plane motor on the field had been cut off after warming up. Through the enveloping background of the silence itself he could hear occasionally the faint purring of the bowser engines pumping to replace in the plane tanks every drop of the precious gallons expended in the warming up of the motors.

Dennis had been raising his wrist watch closer to his eyes when he heard them. There was an explosion of muffled coughing padded with the whirring of starters. Then the reports deepened as motors caught. The noise blended rapidly into a cup of continuous thunder that pressed in around him from every side. The air, the roof, his clothes, his body, the universe itself, began to shake with a thunder of vibrations rising up and ever up beyond every former crescendo of man's imagining.

Around him the grayness of the mist tossed and danced in fitful homeless dislocation, swirling and opening and closing, lifting and falling and eddying in a demented frenzy of disintegration that tore the physical texture of the air. Then, through the turbulence, he had

199

seen the spectral fans of the riding lights rolling around the perimeter track toward him.

The great beetles waddled heavily as they came. Through the thunder itself cut the gnatlike squealing of brakes protesting the crushing momentum of bomb and gas loads. They came faster, running a little to catch up with each other and then checking themselves with clumsy jerks and half turns. As the leader stopped the others pressed in behind it, inching and squeezing for compression, jealous of every foot of space between them with its inexorable price of gas to be burned for recovery of their final position in the air.

The compressed waiting line zigzagged back into the mist which had become heavy with the acrid fumes of burning brake bands. Down the line Dennis could see the faces of the pilots and copilots and discern the drawn tension under the long visors even through the blur of universal vibration. Some wiped endlessly with waste at the vapor on the plexiglass before them, some craned their necks anxiously out of windows before closing up another few inches.

From long habit Dennis counted as they came. The brakes on the last one were still squealing when he saw the blink of the Ops light. The heavy thunder of the column had abated now for economy of fuel. With the blinking of that light it broke over him again in all the final fury of the force that beat down gravity itself.

The lead plane lifted visibly in its tracks against the rigidity of its brakes. The naked girl on the nose blurred, even her most prominent points of interest dissolving into one quivering pale blob of light against mottled green darkness. Mist leaped upward in flight from the

200

thunder of the whole column. Through the sudden clarity Dennis saw space opening behind the lead ship, and saw that she was receding from him.

He had known that Ted should be busy at the radio desk. As always Dennis had driven Martin out to the parking stand in his own car. This morning the young pilot had had his crew drawn up at rigid attention to await them, his eager face almost bursting with pride over their passenger.

"Good morning, sir. Would you like to go over anything?"

"Not with you, Luther," Martin had grinned. "Better tell 'em to get in."

They had both felt a reflex of the pleasure in the compliment as the crew scrambled rapidly out of sight. Martin had walked forward for a studious scrutiny of the girl on the nose before nodding approval.

"She could fly us home with those in a pinch, Casey."

"Well, take care of 'em, Ted."

"Yeah."

They never shook hands. Martin had glanced once more at his watch, winked, and stepped briskly toward the hatch when he had stopped and turned back, the grin gone from his face.

"Casey, keep your head with that Congress, will you?"

"Sure. You keep your feet dry, Ted."

Now as the blurred flesh-colored blob of the girl rolled down the strip away from him, Dennis saw the young pilot's arm flash in farewell to him. He waved back at the boy with emotion.

The plane gathered way rapidly; in three seconds she

201

was rolling lightly. He strained his eyes, still waving as she began to lift into the mist itself, and at the last second he clearly saw a new figure and another arm suddenly flash from the left waistgate. It comforted him.

He had remained on the roof for most of the next hour, his ears attuned to every vibration of the laborious struggle for altitude and formation, tracing them round and round the shrouded perimeter of the horizon above him. Every circle told its own story of tighter harmony in the throbbing as the last planes off closed up with the first ones and the universal thunder diminished imperceptibly into a high, far drone.

Three times he had held his breath over the sudden blossoming of rockets, discernible even through the mist, but there had been no collisions that morning. Upward and ever upward the diminishing drone corkscrewed away from him. For a time it gained in unity what it lost in proximity while Martin shepherded them expertly together. But the time passed.

As their physical presence receded Dennis had felt again the familiar weight of anxiety descending upon him. The ground commander, delivering battle, can feel his way in, probing with a tentative, ordered sequence of patrols, platoons, companies, battalions. It is almost always his option to terminate the engagement if it appears unfavorable. Similarly naval forces feel for each other with expendable tentacles before deliberately accepting irrevocable commitment.

The offensive bomber force, crossing water, burns the bridges of retreat in its own gas tanks. Every maneuver of battle narrows the margin of its return. But even beyond battle itself lurk hazards of an equally final disaster. An unforeseen change of wind, a serious navigational mistake or careless use of fuel for flight, can force down an entire formation into grounded captivity.

Dennis and Martin had spent long hours with able help, weighing the problems of wind, weather, altitude, speed, and daylight against the counterclaims of flak, fighters, and fatigue. Always the intermediate specter of disaster hovered over each beguiling illusion about the shortest distance between two points. They had emerged with a margin over which they had looked at each other in shocked silence until Martin had burst out laughing.

"I'm going to take my toothbrush."

Gradually as Dennis listened through the gray mist the arcs of the sound became wider and wider. Once more it came back with a slight rise of force and that time as it began to recede he knew it was fading with the finality of the course. He was starting heavily into the Ops room when a last indulgence of nature rewarded his long vigil.

For a fleeting second some capricious zephyr parted the mist and he had a brief view of the whole column, already miles above him. The upward angles of the early sun had caught their wings and bellies, paling the young daylight they cleft with an arching chain of iridescence.

They were still badly spread out. Ted would not waste a drop of gas to hurry the agonizing process of formation but they had taken their easterly heading. The long, loose procession spangled the sky with an arrowy scintillation, through a brief and final gleam, before Dennis stood alone again in the heavy mist their vibrations no longer troubled. He became aware of silence now as he had then and realized that Mr. Malcolm was repeating a question to him.

"Are they undeh fighteh coveh today, Gennel?"

"Not all the way. Fighters will take them to here . . ." he indicated the final turnback point on the map . . . "and another relay will pick them up here, coming out. They'll be on their own the rest of the way."

"An' you sent them on youah own authority again?"

"Yes."

"Is theah any reason why you cain't fin' woyth-while tahgets undeh fighteh coveh like the otheh gennels do?"

"These extension tanks were made to enable us to reach the most important targets in their range. We're doing it."

"You just sen' 'em regahdless of fighteh coveh?"

"I thought I'd explained, Mr. Malcolm, that our present fighters can't reach these targets."

"You ain't explained why you puhsonally are the onlies' one to sen' 'em beyon' fighteh coveh every time Gennel Kane got his back turned on otheh business. Neah as I can figuah out more than half the losses of this whole Aih Ahmy come out of these heah recohd attacks fum this one division. Lemme see that tonnage an' sohtie chaht again, Sahgeant."

Evans produced the chart grudgingly. He had cherished the illusion of independence for many years but he knew now that he had come to the end of it. In the army, of all places, and to a General, of all human beings, he had come at last to the common burden of allegiance.

There was pride in it, pride that had made him whisper to himself: *I bet Dennis makes him sorry he ever stuck his head out of the swamp.* But there was pain in it too, the certain pain of the price Dennis would pay for this pleasure.

"I thought so," said Malcolm. "Every otheh division has consistently increased sohties an' tonnages excep' . . ."

"If you're interested in sortie and tonnage figures, Mr. Malcolm," said Dennis, "I suggest you visit the training commands. They beat all the operational commands combined — that is, all but the training commands in your state."

"What are you sayin' about my state?"

"That every airfield in it is under eighteen inches of water half the year and four to nine thousand feet of solid overcast for nine months. But every time we tried to move somewhere we could operate the recommendations were blocked in your committee."

Evans held his breath but unexpectedly the open laughter of Stone and Field checked the smoldering combustion in the room long enough for Kane to intervene.

"You're straying from the subject, General. We all realize, Mr. Malcolm, that the country expects a rising scale of effort from us. We still have tomorrow to bring our monthly totals of sorties and tonnages to a new record high. It would be a great thing for public confidence if your delegation here were to make the announcement. I'm sure we can clear it with the Chief and I'm sure that Brockie here will help us with the press."

"Are you?" asked Brockhurst pointedly.

"Of course," said Kane.

Brockhurst subsided but Malcolm knew appeasement when he heard it.

"I'm suah that will help, Gennel. But the announcement the public is really waitin' foh is the end of these muhderous long-range attacks. If I have anything to say about it . . ."

"This division's operations are determined by military directive, Mr. Malcolm," said Dennis.

Malcolm turned truculently on Dennis and Evans's heart lifted. The Congressman was formidably larger than the General. One hostile gesture would justify any soldier's defense of his superior. Evans eyed the Congressman's crotch with an eager twitching in his heavy shoe. He had never found occasion to use all his army education but the prospects looked promising. They were spoiled for the moment, however, by the entrance of Haley.

"Red and blue forces now approaching objectives, sir."

Chapter Twelve

AS ALWAYS the claim of the operation swept everything else from Dennis's mind. He had forgotten the Congressman towering above him at the first sight of Haley.

"Getting any reaction?"

"Not yet, sir," said Haley reluctantly, "but they should bomb in about two minutes and a half."

"Gentlemen," said Kane, "I'm going to take you down to the radar plotting and signals room myself, but you will probably understand what you're seeing better if General Dennis gives us a quick résumé on this map first."

Dennis made short work of explaining the problem on which he had spent most of the night. Through this his visitors followed him attentively with sensible questions. Seen as three lines on a map the problem looked simple. He omitted all mention of the compounding factors of time correlation and gas consumption.

The details of the defenses appeared equally simple. It took little experience to see how quickly German fighters could converge from either side against that center course, how relatively few were the groups on the extremities that might, with luck, be lured into wasting effort on Endicott's and Salmond's short stabs in from the protective vastness of their ocean approach and withdrawal courses.

"When will your Fifth Division bomb, General?" asked Field.

"About fourteen minutes now, sir."

"And these other missions are essentially a diversion to prevent concentration of the defenses against your division?"

"They serve two purposes," said Kane quickly. "They are attacking very important naval objectives. But of course they will help to split the defenses."

"Do you expect their diversionary purpose to succeed, General Dennis?" asked Stone.

"Not entirely unless they've got a green controller on duty. It may help a little; it's the best we could do."

"Gentlemen, General Dennis will not wish to leave his office just now. If you'll come with me we'll rejoin him presently," said Kane.

It was a novelty to be forbidden his own plotting room, however subtly, but the order was unmistakable. Dennis watched them file out with a feeling of relief. But as the last of them stepped through the door and Haley began to lead them down the winding steps to the bombproof nerve center far underground, Kane lingered in the office, his aplomb collapsing in a frantic concern that ignored the presence of Evans.

"Casey, for Christ's sake be careful . . ."

"Sir, you promised me Fendelhorst tomorrow. . . ."

"By tomorrow Malcolm could have us both in the Quartermaster Corps in Greenland. Is that citation ready?"

"Yes, sir."

"And a good lunch?"

"Yes, sir."

"And plenty to drink?"

"Why . . . I hadn't thought of it, sir. . . ."

"Hadn't thought of booze with Congressmen here? For God's sake start thinking . . . in double triples."

He closed the door and fled after the party. Dennis allowed some of his indignation to explode into speech before he noticed Evans.

"*Booze!* It's a goddamned wonder he doesn't want opium and slave girls!"

"We can start them on benzedrine and Wacs, sir. Regular field conditions," said Evans.

"Evans, is there plenty in the officers' bar?"

"Not a drop, sir."

"What?"

"End of the month, sir. Quota's gone."

"Nothing?"

"Local beer, sir. I suppose Congressmen would drink it but . . ."

"How about the Medical Officer?"

"He hasn't been paid back for the time those Cabinet members were here, sir. He's still dry."

"God damn democracy!" said Dennis.

"Sir, there are the combat ration stocks."

"They're low, aren't they?"

"Enough for about six missions left, sir."

Dennis thought but not for long. "All right. These bastards can go dry for one day. Maybe it'll kill them."

"Sir, General Kane ordered . . ."

"Damn it, Sergeant, I can't sweat whiskey, can I?"

"Sir, just a little from the combat stocks . . ."

"Not a drop. Now get the hell out of here. . . ."

"I knew there was a catch in this job," said Evans.

Dennis watched with speechless stupefaction as the Sergeant, in direct disobedience of his order, walked

209

calmly to the Division Flag Locker, unsnapped the pad-lock and, reaching inside, pulled out some bottles of excellent bourbon whiskey.

"Sergeant, where on earth . . . ?"

"Present from an admirer, sir. It's too good for the Congress but if we have to . . ."

"Look here . . ." said Dennis. He pulled out his wallet, grateful for an excuse to cover his emotion. "You could get . . ."

"No, sir." Evans put the whiskey on the map table and shook his head with finality at the money. Then, a little hesitantly, he spoke again. "I'd like one thing for it, sir."

"What?"

"To shake your hand."

Dennis extended a hand with the feeling that this transaction was becoming more improper every minute and a scandalized realization that he did not give a damn.

"What's this for, Sergeant?"

"For telling that servant of the people what a son of a bitch he is," said Evans.

"Oh . . . well, you'd better get some glasses and water."

But as he reached the door Evans heard the General's voice again. For the first time in his recollection it was not entirely steady.

"Sergeant, I appreciate this."

"Well, sir, I'd hate . . . breaking in a new general."

Haley, returning from the hole, found Dennis staring at the whiskey on the map table with a warmth in his face the Colonel had never seen.

"Well?"

"Not a blip, sir. The Krauts are wise today. I'm afraid Ted's getting the whole dose."

"Nothing from him yet, of course?"

"He's not due for eleven minutes, sir. General Kane is showing his visitors around downstairs. I have some figures."

They were deep in arithmetic at the board when Garnett hurried into the office.

"Casey, the Old Man says for God's sake . . ."

"Just a minute, Cliff. Hurry up, Haley."

". . . and twenty-six of yesterday's battle damage. . . ."

Watching the concentration with which Dennis agonized over every detail, Garnett wondered now how he could ever have envied him. Kane's original choice between them had bitterly disappointed Garnett. At the time it had been the best air command in the war for a brigadier and the whole service knew it.

Duty with the United Chiefs, however, had brought Garnett compensations. There had been time to study and analyze the whole war. He had lived with invaluable foreknowledge of what was going to happen. Now, with momentous B-29 commands on the near horizon, Garnett could bless the decision that had fixed Dennis so firmly here and left himself in a position of unique advantage.

The specter of German jets, overhanging the already precarious position of this command, accentuated Garnett's gratitude for his personal detachment from it. He understood the gravity of the threat and he admired the courage of Dennis's response to it. But Garnett had seen enough of the highest echelons to know that they re-

211

quired more than courage from subordinate commanders. In the military world as elsewhere men sought and cherished subordinates whose successes seemed to reflect the brighter gleams of a favorable fortune.

Success with the countermeasure of Stitch would be an invisible success, won at gruesome cost. Failure would discredit American Air Power in this theater, dislocate the timetable, possibly reverse Global Strategy. For there was powerful opinion that the B-29's, under the right command, could be decisive in the Pacific.

"... so we should be able to count on a margin of thirty-eight."

"Thanks," said Dennis. "Send Davis with the noon map."

As Haley scuttled out Dennis apologized to Garnett.

"Sorry, Cliff. I had to get a reading on tomorrow before that traveling circus gets back in here. What's up?"

"The Old Man wants you to be more careful with the visiting Elks. Between ourselves, he's scared, Casey."

"Yeah." Garnett thought Dennis looked more sad than contemptuous. "A man who's held altitude records, scared of Congressmen."

"Confidentially, Casey, he knows he's pretty close to that third star."

"I wonder if that's where it sets in?" Dennis smiled. "Let me know, will you?"

"You'll be likelier to let *me* know, with your record now."

"Don't kid me," said Dennis. "Haven't you got one of those B-29 jobs sewed up?"

Garnett managed a deprecatory laugh: "I thought so

till I suddenly got shunted over here without explanation. Of course it's only an observation tour but some of that Washington competition is pretty rough. You're well out of it, Casey."

This time he could see that Dennis was trying to cover a smile. It served him right. There was no use beating around the bush with a man who knew this business as well as he did.

"Listen, old man, did Ted speak to you about this?"

"No."

"Well, it wouldn't hurt my chances a bit if the Chief knew he'd like to be my chief of staff out there."

"Did you talk to him about it?"

"Casey, it isn't proselytizing when a guy's your own brother-in-law. It isn't your fault, but we both know you'll never be able to give him more than Eagles in this job."

"What can you give him?"

"One star immediately. And the Pacific looks like a long war."

"Did he know this last night?"

"Yes."

Garnett watched tautly while Dennis looked first at his watch and then intently at the map.

"I wish I had."

"I realize it was . . . unorthodox of me to speak to him first, but you know yourself you have to handle Ted with kid gloves."

Dennis appeared to be thinking this over for so long that Garnett was on the verge of elaborating when the reply came.

213

"Cliff, just don't try to handle him. He does that fine."

"You mean . . . it's all right . . . I can have him?"

"For that job? Of course."

"And you'll . . . persuade him?"

"Yes."

"Casey, if you knew what this means to me . . ."

"Save it, Cliff. I'm not doing it for you."

Garnett gulped and recovered fast. There was no rancor in the reply but Dennis had withdrawn into his shell.

"You don't understand. I'm thanking you for Ted, old man."

"I'm not doing it for him entirely. Those B-29's need Ted."

"Don't worry, Casey, we'll make 'em sing. After the example you fellows have given us over here . . ."

Haley and Davis returned with the weather map and at first sight of them Dennis forgot everything else. He had spread the map on the table and was already scrutinizing it before he spoke again.

"Well . . . ?"

"The mass is denser but that's slowing it up, sir. It's eighty-four miles behind expected drift now."

"How much longer will that give us?"

"The Continent will be cavu all day, sir. But at present drift this will start closing the bases in by fifteen hundred."

"How would that fit, Haley?"

"Lacks about twenty minutes, sir."

Dennis nodded and walked a slow circle around the room, deep in thought. Garnett glanced at the map.

"Can't you just start them that much earlier?"

Dennis did not answer. Haley coughed apologetically.

"It would mean forming in the dark . . . with that gas and bomb load. We have observed that sometimes early collisions have a demoralizing effect upon a whole mission, sir."

Dennis came back to the table, still oblivious of Garnett.

"But even by sixteen hundred they could clearly see where the island is from, say, fifteen thousand?"

"Yes, sir," said Davis. "It'll stack up over the island like froth on a beer till it cools enough to move on. That's the trouble."

"Bring me the fourteen hundred map as soon as it's done and anything special as it comes. Haley, wait a minute."

Dennis waited until the door closed on Davis.

"Have every spare parachute in the Division repacked this afternoon. Tonight repack enough from the Groups till you can fill out with fresh packs tomorrow."

Garnett saw Haley stiffen with the impact of the order but his discipline did not fail him. He replied with a steady "Yes, sir," and left the room at once.

"Casey, what are you thinking of?"

"Paratroops do it."

"But the planes . . ."

"They're expendable, Cliff."

"A whole division for one target?"

"All they're made for is to hit the right targets."

"But have you thought what they'll say in Washington?"

"I'm thinking what they'll say in Berlin. They count on weather like this."

215

2

Brockhurst, entering just then, could not be sure whether he saw or only wished to see that Garnett was staring at Dennis with an awed respect. He decided that it was imagination. It was the essence of the whole ghastly tragedy that none of the little men whom the accidents of rank had placed around Dennis ever would understand him. In all fairness Brockhurst had to acknowledge that only yesterday he himself had thought Dennis a blundering butcher.

"General Garnett, General Kane asked me to ask you if you would come down to the hole at once."

He watched Garnett spring for the door with the instinctive, unthinking obedience that was at once the strength and the ruin of the service. Dennis put on the formality with which he always shielded himself from strangers.

"Did General Kane want me?"

"No," said Brockhurst, "nor me either. That's the point."

He had hoped to invite curiosity and through it a moment of intimacy for personal amends, but the next remark showed him what he should have known; Dennis did not rise to civilian innuendoes.

"Did he tell you to loaf in here?"

"General, I owe you a personal apology."

"These are my working hours, Mr. Brockhurst."

"You see, General Kane has double-crossed me. . . ."

"Please take your grievance against my boss to him."

"But that's not what's important. He's double-crossing you."

"You're speaking of my superior, Mr. Brockhurst."

"He's ordering a recall signal on your mission."

This did shake that stony impassivity. Dennis glanced at his watch and then at the map, but his lips remained locked.

"I know it's too late to save losses," said Brockhurst. "They're probably fighting now. But it puts Kane on record. What happens now is your rap."

"And my business," said Dennis evenly.

"It's the country's business, if the country could know. He's sacrificing the whole operation, taking the losses without getting the result . . . just from fear."

"Commanders have to fear losses, Mr. Brockhurst."

Momentarily Dennis had become more responsive than the correspondent had ever known him. But the armor of his uniform still seemed impenetrable.

"He isn't afraid of losses and you know it. He isn't afraid of Germany or Washington or even these god-damned Congressmen. There's only one thing in the world Kane is afraid of now and that's you."

"Me?" At least the surprise was genuine.

"You. Because you're doing what's right and Kane has lived long enough to know that someone always pays a hell of a price for that."

"The boys are paying that, Mr. Brockhurst."

"Not all of it. Kane's got you framed like a picture."

Dennis spoke patiently, as if to a troublesome child. "You don't understand the army."

"It's only people in uniform. I understand people."

"No it isn't. People only shout for soldiers after they've blundered themselves into danger they can't cope with as people. Then they accept the uniform. . . ."

"Nuts. Even military decisions have to be made on the opinions of men. When you know yours are right . . ."

"It's your duty to persuade your superior as forcibly as you can. After that it's your duty to execute his decision."

"Even when you know he's shirking the decision?"

"You don't know it. He may be acting on information you don't have. This whole bombardment program may be only a diversion or holding attack in the higher strategy. I'm paid to serve General Kane; others are paid to judge him."

"You have faith they're better at the top?"

"We keep chaplains for questions of faith, Mr. Brockhurst."

"You keep everything; you've got it all taped, haven't you? Your own chaplains, judge advocates, food, pay, promotion, decoration, and unlimited free coffins . . . you've made a separate world out of it with everything a man . . ."

"Everything but freedom" — Dennis smiled wryly now — "but I've read, in your press, that we're fighting for that."

"And your personal part in this . . ."

"Is very simple. Life without freedom is. I am responsible for making this command inflict maximum injury on the enemy, within orders."

"And when the orders are deliberately ambiguous?"

"Your superior may be receiving the same kind."

Brockhurst nodded wearily. "Okay, General, you get

a hundred on the rules. But don't ask me to think you believe in them against everything in reason . . ."

"That's what war is, Mr. Brockhurst. If we win, reason may get another chance."

The teleprinter in the next room burst into frenzied clattering now and its first accents claimed Dennis with instant reversion to the harsh reality of the mission. Brockhurst watched him disappear through the door.

Brockhurst realized, as he knew Dennis had, that Kane's recall signal to the mission marked a turning point. Up to then the senior commander had, at least negatively, countenanced Dennis's course of action. Now he had made mechanical preparation for an adroit jettison. It was plain premeditated dissociation from the risk he had permitted Dennis to take.

Yet Brockhurst knew now that the foreseeable fate of Dennis was only a fragment, a shadow of the larger catastrophe he was witnessing. Dennis himself was safely beyond pity. Brockhurst's brief glimpse inside the uniform had shown him a man who could carry himself, as he carried his convictions, inviolable through momentary changes of fortune.

The darker tragedy hid behind the form of Dennis, behind the army itself. The army was only the projected form of a deeper malignance. It had been created as a shield against a more highly developed tyranny than its own; it would survive by a superior ferocity.

It was futile to pity Dennis, to hate Kane, to rage at his own helplessness in the face of the army's bestial stupidity and human venality; they were all manifestations of what had made them. It was not the weaknesses, the faults, the mistakes of armies; it was their existence that proclaimed the tragedy of mankind.

Chapter Thirteen

　　AS GENERAL KANE'S PARTY returned from the hole Malcolm paused on the threshold of the door, pointing like a bird dog while a beaming, beatific grin overspread his heavy face.

"Drinkin' whiskey fum Gawd's own country!"

He hurried to the bar which Evans had improvised on the map table and raised a bottle for critical inspection.

"Gennel Kane, I declah youah a min' readeh. Wheah in the worl' did you get this oveh heah?"

Kane hesitated but Evans did not. "It was a present to General Dennis from an admirer, sir."

Brockhurst noticed the whiskey for the first time now. A rueful grin spread over his face.

"Yes, Sergeant, it is," he said.

The others thronged forward to it eagerly. Kane made the most of the prevailing satisfaction to report to Dennis what he had done, covering his evident sense of unease with formality.

"General, as you know I pride myself on never interfering with normal operations. But today's diversions were so obviously unsuccessful that I felt it my duty to signal Colonel Martin discretion to abandon his primary objective for a target of opportunity under fighter cover if he chose."

"Did you get a reply, sir?" asked Dennis evenly.

"Not yet. He's probably preserving radio silence."

Prescott appeared now with a glass for Kane. Over by the bar Brockhurst was watching with amusement the completion of a cycle. For intent as they were upon the whiskey, the Congressmen had not allowed it to eclipse their own horizons. Discovering Evans no longer in mute attendance upon Kane, they had turned to the earnest courtship of the potential voter in the Sergeant's bemedaled blouse.

". . . an' may I ask which of ouah great states has the honoh of producin' a man whose country has rewahded him with medals like them?" inquired Malcolm.

"You can but I'd rather not say," said Evans.

"Not say! You mean you ain't proud of youah home state?"

"I wasn't till I saw what some of the others put out."

"I declah! Gennel, youah Sahgen's not only a *he*ro; he's a wit. Come on, tell us wheah you fum, son."

"If I did you'd quit sucking around for my next vote."

Dennis looked at his watch.

"General Kane, we've had relays from General Endicott and General Salmond. Both report their targets successfully attacked."

"Gentlemen," said Kane hastily, "we have had very gratifying strike reports from the other missions. To two very successful attacks."

He raised his glass and the others joined him heartily. Malcolm handed his back to Evans with careful instructions for refilling it before he turned on Dennis.

"You don't drink to youah colleagues' success, Gennel?"

221

"I'm waiting to drink to the whole operation. Did you enjoy the hole, gentlemen?"

"I was fascinated but I was bewildered, too," said Field.

"It was impressive but too much for the layman," said Stone.

"They wasn't nothin' to it but them girls at the tables movin' little pieces of cahdboahd an' them damn shoht-circuit spahks on the screen an' the whole place coldeh than Chris'mas."

Malcolm shivered and took more whiskey in a long gulp. Brockhurst saw both Dennis and Kane look at their watches now. Even through his modest share of his own whiskey he could feel tension tightening in the room. He saw Dennis start visibly as the teleprinter suddenly began to clatter again in the Ops room, but Stone had pinned the Brigadier down with earnest questioning.

"But we did understand, correctly, that the main purpose of these other attacks was diversionary?"

"They were very important naval objectives," said Kane quickly. "Of course we did hope to split the enemy fighters."

"And you considered that hope had failed, General?"

Kane hesitated perceptibly. "You can't be certain. But the screen is reasonably accurate at that range and the technicians identified no fighters. What do you think, General?"

"The other strike signals would have mentioned any significant scale of fighting, sir."

"So you had to assume, in fact, that the main enemy forces are free to strike our central attack?"

"We had to assume it to begin with, sir," said Den-

222

nis. "The diversions were only a hope — the best we could do, but still a hope."

"Well," persisted Stone, "if the main force had already gone so far . . ."

"You mean *been sent* so far," said Malcolm. He had brought his glass over to join the argument now and his voice had taken on truculence with the whiskey. "An' it had been sent by Gennel Dennis when he knew his own self that his divehsions probably wouldn't succeed. Am I not correct, Gennel?"

"You are."

Haley appeared in the doorway with teleprint paper in his hand.

"Liaison message from an R.A.F. recce plane, sir."

"Read it."

Haley lifted the paper and read aloud, his flat unemotional accents falling like stones into the silence.

" 'Twelve hundred thirty-nine sighted large formation of USAAF Boeings approx ten forty east fifty forty north altitude twenty-two thousand heading ninety-eight . . .' "

"Ninety-eight!" exclaimed Kane. "He's still going *into* Germany!"

Haley waited but no one spoke. He resumed: " 'unescorted under heavy attack formations good over.' That's all, sir."

He executed a sharp about-face and closed the door behind him, muffling a little the teleprinter, which had begun to clatter again. The men looked at each other blankly, heavily. Dennis lifted an eye from his wrist watch for a long look at the map. It was Malcolm who broke the silence. The liquor was dissolving the thin

223

restraint over his natural volatility; he sounded nearly hysterical.

". . . unescohted an' undeh heavy attack. Gennel Kane, I'm wahnin' you if you eveh let Gennel Dennis . . ."

"Aaathur, you better shut up," said Stone.

"I agree," said Field. "If they think it necessary. . . !"

"Necessary! To slaughteh American youth foh one pigheaded Brigadieh . . ."

He was walking toward Dennis again. Evans quietly stepped to the side of the table, his foot itching hopefully again when, unconsciously, they all froze with the cessation of sound from the teleprinter, the quick rasp of tearing paper, and then the approaching beat of Haley's feet. Entering, he looked uncertainly at Dennis.

"Message for you, sir."

"From Ted?"

"Not exactly, sir. Could you step out here?"

Dennis started for the door but Malcolm blocked him.

"No you don't, neitheh. You don't play no back room games on me. Weah heah representin' the whole people an' I'm goin' to heah the whole story . . ."

"Colonel, read the message aloud," barked Kane hastily.

Haley stepped through the door and read as unemotionally as before.

" 'Relay on administrative cable from message center London for Colonel Edward Martin in clear new copilot made first successful landing four-fourteen this morning everything fine Helen.' There is no 'over' sir, but they sometimes omit it on administrative messages," said Haley apologetically.

Brockhurst saw the strain in Dennis's face break into the first elation he had ever seen there.

"Jesus! Ted's got a son." He strode over to Garnett and extended a hand, his smile widening. "Congratulations, uncle!"

The Congressmen reacted to the news with a unanimous and purposeful convergence upon the bar. Prescott brought Kane another drink and even Haley unbent for comment.

"I imagine the Colonel and Mrs. Martin will be pleased."

"Gentlemen," said Kane. "Colonel Martin's son."

The others raised their glasses. Dennis spoke quietly to Haley.

"Get a copy ready to relay to Ted in the clear, Haley."

"It's being done, sir."

"But don't send it till we hear."

"No, sir."

"Till you hear what?" demanded Malcolm.

"His strike flash. It's due very soon now."

"You tellin' me this cunnel out theah leadin' the attack been bohn a daddy an' you ain't even goin' to tell him . . ."

"He needs his mind on his work now."

"Gennel Kane, this the mos' inhuman thing . . ."

But to Evans's continuing disappointment Kane himself now appeared to be disgusted with the Congressman; his answer was short.

"General Dennis is right. Colonel Martin must have gone ahead, on his own judgment, of course. How long do you make it now, General?"

"Seven if we're right on the wind, sir."

Kane nodded and summoned a conciliatory smile for the Congressmen.

"Fortunately, gentlemen, war also has its pleasant duties. We have just time for one of them now. General Dennis, will you ask for your adjutant and Captain Jenks?"

Brockhurst thought for a second that Dennis might refuse. For the briefest perceptible interval he appeared to be considering whether or not to obey. Then habit won. He turned swiftly to the Operations room. As he did Evans left the bar and stuck his head into the anteroom.

"Let's go, boys," he said.

2

In response to Evans's request there now appeared from the anteroom three stalwart young soldiers. They were heavily armed with cameras and they swaggered with the arrogance men always take from the possession of significant weapons. Congressmen and soldiers alike made way for them and stood uneasily, adjusting blouses and ties, moving forward or back, meekly eyeing lenses and flashlight bulbs and the businesslike preparations of the young men.

In through the other door the Adjutant strutted with a sheaf of papers and a little box. Behind him, still sullen but clean-shaven now and clad in a be-ribboned blouse

226

and freshly pressed pinks, came Captain Jenks. He hesitated for one nervous glance at Dennis but the Brigadier had stepped quietly into the background and did not speak.

The Adjutant arranged himself and Jenks before Kane, who had taken up a position with both eyes studying the cameramen. The Congressmen maneuvered themselves into a happy position, facing the lenses through the opening between Jenks and Kane.

"Is everything . . . ?" queried Kane sharply.

"You're okay, General. Just pull that blouse down a little," said the head cameraman.

Kane smoothed the blouse around his hips, shot a quick glance around him, and cleared his throat.

"Gentlemen, few experiences in life are more gratifying than according proper recognition to a man who has fought for his country. Will Captain Jenks please step forward?"

Captain Jenks did. The soldiers raised their cameras, the room quieted with an expectant hush, and the Adjutant began to read from the paper in his hand.

"Captain Lucius Malcolm Jenks, for outstandingly meritorious and heroic achievement . . ."

"Excuse me, General," interrupted Evans.

"*WHAT?* . . ." Kane regarded the Sergeant with impatience.

"Would the gentlemen from Congress like to put their glasses over here before the boys start photographing?"

The gentlemen from Congress looked at their glasses as if they held snakes, before marching solemnly around to deposit them on the map table. The camera detail now made ostentatious motions to assure the whole company that no lens would record the spectacle of that table. As the Congressmen returned to their positions Malcolm stopped, with a sudden chuckle, and clapped Evans on the back.

"You goin' a long way in life, boy."

Stone and Field muttered a somewhat more subdued gratitude and followed Malcolm toward the perspective of the lenses. The Adjutant surveyed them all with an expression of pain and began again.

Brockhurst did not follow the details of the citation. His first perceptive glance between Jenks and that little box in the Adjutant's hand had filled in the last piece of the puzzle. He knew now how Dennis had done it. Briefly there stirred in him a hope that Dennis had extracted a promise of personal protection for himself as part of this diabolical bargain. His second thought rejected the idea.

A man who had been thinking of himself would not have driven the bargain. Dennis had been safe before, safe behind military secrecy, safe in the bland, self-protecting unity of the services that would have explained away disaster by jets as calmly as they had explained away Pearl Harbor.

Brockhurst watched him now, standing with silent composure through the enormity of this citation. Twice during the reading he saw Dennis glance briefly at his watch before returning his inscrutable, fixed stare toward the map. Not a flicker of feeling showed on his face as the Adjutant came to the end of his fulsome, rounded periods: —

". . . thereby reflecting great credit upon Captain

228

Jenks and the Army Air Forces, in consideration of which and for his example, achievements and contributions to the advancement of American Aerial Bombardment, Captain Jenks is hereby awarded . . ."

Kane lifted that famous jaw a trifle, glanced once more toward the cameras, and then, accepting the medal from the Adjutant, pinned it upon Jenks. An explosion of flashlight bulbs dazzled the room. Malcolm burst from the formation of Congressmen, threw his arm around his nephew, and accosted Kane eagerly.

"By God, Gennel, this the proudes' moment of ouah lives. Do you reckon . . . ?"

"Of course," said Kane. "You have plenty of film, boys?"

"Plenty. You better get a little closer, General."

The trio arranged themselves, Kane centered between the other two and clasping their hands for a new barrage.

"You gettin' this, Elmeh, boy?" asked Malcolm.

"I'm beginning to get it," said Brockhurst.

They posed twice more before Kane's roving, restless eyes noticed the other two Congressmen standing quietly together away from the cameras. He hurried over to them.

"Gentlemen, no one of our great states has a monopoly on bravery. This command has personnel drawn from every state in the Union. It is my hope, and intention, that before you leave here each one of you may participate in one of these ceremonies."

The Congressmen kept their faces straight.

"Well, General," said Stone, "if one of our boys should happen . . ."

229

"These things mean a lot to morale on the home front," said Field.

"You may rest assured, gentlemen . . ."

Malcolm had led Jenks to the bar. He broke in loudly now, holding up a tumbler half full of whiskey.

"Gentlemen, a toas' to the boy who led his squadron . . ."

He stopped, as the whole room stopped in every motion, frozen by the sibylline clatter of the teleprinter. There was the rasp of tearing paper, and again Haley was at the door, handing an inch-wide strip of paper to Dennis. The Brigadier looked at it intently for several seconds before reading aloud: —

" 'No mistake this time. Scratch Schweinhafen for me. Ted.' "

For a second more he stared at it silently and then before their eyes seemed to explode with exultation.

"Jesus, Haley, he got it . . . *he got it* . . . HE GOT IT!"

"Yes, sir," said Haley. "Colonel Martin is a very determined man."

Throughout the whole room now the tension broke into a tumult of happy chatter. The others crowded forward for a look at the paper itself.

"Signal him about his kid, Haley."

"It's going out, sir."

Garnett raised a glass, his face jubilant and glowing with pride.

"Gentlemen, the greatest combat leader in the Army Air Forces. Fill 'em up."

Only Malcolm seemed unaffected by the general elation. He was standing by Jenks at the bar, still holding the glass he had raised in abortive toast to his nephew, and his voice was petulant.

"Gennel, was this heah Schweinhafen any fahtheh than my nephew's mission to Posenleben?"

Kane hesitated. "Well, perhaps a little farther in miles . . ."

But Prescott had seen the General's embarrassment.

"Sir, I don't like to delay the toasts but Colonel Martin has asked us to scratch Schweinhafen for him. It occurs to me that while the photographers are here . . ."

He proffered a piece of red crayon. Kane seized it and strode happily toward the map while the photographers took up new positions. Then, as he was raising his arm, Kane caught himself.

"Gentlemen, it would be a great thing for public confidence . . ."

The last of his invitation was drowned in the stampede as the Congressmen swarmed to him now, straightening ties and putting down glasses. Prescott was maneuvering them into position when through the half-open door they heard a muffled: "Christ!" in Haley's heavy voice. His face was streaming tears as he walked in and handed another inch of paper to Dennis.

Dennis took one look; then the paper fell from his hand and he stepped away from the others, turning his back on them. It was Garnett who picked it up and made himself read aloud: —

" 'Good luck, Casey. We're on fire and going . . .' "

He stopped, staring at it strickenly. Only Malcolm could not stand the silence; his heavy panting burst into a scream.

"Goin'. . . ? Goin' wheah? Finish it, cain't you?"

"That's all there is."

"Awll . . . ? *Awll* . . . ?"

They saw hysteria possess him but no one could stir as he walked over and whirled Dennis angrily around by the shoulder.

"You mean to tell me he's . . . ?"

"Shut up!"

"Shut up? You standin' theah an' tellin' me to shut up afteh you've done kilt . . ."

Evans had started for him but not fast enough. They scarcely saw Dennis move but the impact of his fist thudded. Malcolm lifted as if in slow motion and then collapsed over backward with a resounding crash. As he hit the floor the whiskey in his hand spilled over him, darkening the lavender shirt with a widening ring of stain. He did not stir. Slowly the glass rolled off him and came to rest gently on the floor beside his unconscious body.

The others stared dazedly but Evans snatched a camera. Training it on the prostrate Malcolm, he addressed Dennis quietly.

"You want a picture of the battle damage, sir?"

His voice broke the tension. Kane stepped over to Evans, grabbed the camera, and smashed it on the floor. He had opened his mouth to speak when the clatter of the teleprinter began to echo through the room again. Kane waited, his mouth hanging open. Dennis was staring down at the Congressman, face impassive as ever, his figure relaxed and steady. Brockhurst noticed a little trickle of blood coming out of the Brigadier's hand. Looking more closely, he saw with surprise the end of a

232

pair of regulation pilot's wings protruding from the clenched fist.

The teleprinter stopped and all eyes turned with conscious dread toward the sound of the tearing paper and approaching feet. This time Haley walked the message straight to General Kane.

"Top secret relay from Washington for you, sir."

Kane read it, gulped, and gathered himself slowly.

"I'm sorry about this, Casey."

Dennis did not answer. He had lifted his eyes from Malcolm to the map and was staring at it, oblivious of everything else. Kane walked over to him and, commanding his attention, read aloud: —

" 'With immediate effect you will replace Brigadier General K. C. Dennis, commanding Fifth Bombardment Division, Heavy, with Brigadier General Clifton C. Garnett, returning General Dennis Washington most expeditious means of transportation.' "

Dennis still showed no sign of having heard it. His eyes were fixed on the map. A drop of blood fell from the cut in his palm. Kane took another long look at him and placed an arm around his shoulder.

"Casey, I'm going to recommend you for the Legion of Merit."

Chapter Fourteen

ELMER BROCKHURST drove out the gate of the Fifth Division early that afternoon with a deeper emotion than he had brought there. He had come the day before with his eye on a story; his heart had been high with hope that he might help the boys, the army, by protecting them from the ruthlessness of General Dennis.

He had remained to learn a new humility, to end his visit with an effort to protect General Dennis from the army. In his new humility he knew that he had been only partially successful. With the support of Field and Stone he had made Malcolm apologize to Dennis. Beyond that he had warned Malcolm against further persecution of Dennis. He had spoken with the power of the press and he knew that Malcolm understood, as Kane had understood and heeded Brockhurst's blunt insistence that the party should leave the station at once.

Against such men the power of the press was effective; for Dennis it was only a trifling, mechanical assistance, the most that Brockhurst or any civilian could now give. For armies and soldiers, as he had known in his heart, could not be helped, even against their own blindness, the blindness that could waste a man like Dennis. Never before had Brockhurst so entirely comprehended that war is waste; that armies are beyond help.

2

Evans entered the office that evening smoldering with a rage that fed on its own futility. Until that moment there had been work, more than enough work, in which to hide his thoughts and feelings. For the army is an inexorable continuity in which the death or transfer of one man is the beginning for another in a structure designed to survive mortality.

Walking to the desk, he removed General Dennis's name plate and replaced it with the new one. Its surfaces were still damp with oiling. The letters spelled Garnett's name.

Evans put the coffee to boil and then, by habit, looked at his watch. There probably wasn't time but he did not care whether he got caught tonight or not. The mechanics of lighting a cigar would prolong his respite from reality a few seconds. He took out the cigar box and then burst into blasphemy at the last barren evidence of the congressional visit. The box was empty. He threw it into the stove and sat down, cornered with the emotions he had been dodging.

Only once before in uniform had he known anything like the sickening finality of this ending. That had been the night his crew broke up after its last mission. Then, however, there had been the incredible realization of survival, the realization that he could now look upon the future as a man with a stake in it, with certain relation to everything in the world which he would continue to inhabit.

This time he wanted to get away from the future but it had him fast. It had him because he was alive again and he was learning that to live is to suffer. He realized now that throughout his entire tour of duty and for some time afterward he had not truly been alive. He had merely functioned mechanically through an existence in which there was no hope, no despair, no feeling whatever. He had understood the odds and had not expected to survive. His existence had been narcotized by the assumption of a cynical indifference toward a world in which he no longer had a stake.

This numbness had persisted into the early stages of his duty with General Dennis. Indeed the first evidence of its thawing had been the sense of concern he had felt over Brockhurst's prophecy that the General would be fired. From that reawakening Evans had passed, in the last twenty-four hours, from amusement to a passionate sympathy and partisanship. Through Dennis he had touched again a high aspiration. With him he had known once more hope and fear, doubt, indignation, triumph, suspense, strife. For him he now felt the despair and frustrate fury with which he regarded everything around him. He had regained the world but it was the world of the army.

Only later, much later, would it occur to a reawakened Evans that it was not the world of the army. It was the world the army had taken in involuntary receivership from the moral and spiritual bankruptcy of its people. It was the world of men like himself who had dodged the draft until danger was on them, of Malcolm and Jenks plotting political profit in the ruins, of Stone and Field dimly perceiving the trouble but impotent to cope with it, of Brockhurst selling the army's secrecy for news copy as all men everywhere now sold it supplies for a living.

Evans would ponder these things later; his reawakening was deep but like all birth shrouded in pain. For the present he knew only that he was still in the army. He would have to deal with this trouble in the army's way. His immediate desire was to get as far from here as he could. Upon arrival he intended to put his new commander in his place at once and keep him there until the unimaginable day when he could tell him to kiss a civilian's ass for a change.

The opening of the door brought him to his feet. Garnett looked better in a woolen shirt. He had either shed some of his pomposity with that well-tailored blouse or the weight of the job was already squeezing it out of him. He was manifestly still nervous but Evans had learned to tolerate this in green commanders.

"Coffee's almost ready, sir," he said.

"I didn't order coffee," said Garnett.

"You will, sir."

Garnett visibly checked a retort and sniffed the air before replying. The familiar smell relaxed him a little.

"Oh, very well, Sergeant."

He went over to his desk now and Evans could see him taking on confidence from the sight of the new name plate.

"Everything in order here, Sergeant?"

"Yes, sir. Benzedrine in top right drawer."

"Oh, Sergeant, can you get sleeping tablets here?"

"I'll see, sir. And you need cigars and whiskey."

"I almost never use them."

237

"It's expected of you, sir."

"By whom?"

"People who do. They're standard equipment for brigadiers in this theater, sir."

Evans did not care what his successor had to smoke or drink but he intended to have no nonsense from Garnett and it was well to begin firmly. Garnett hesitated, manifestly considering the same problem of a firm beginning, but Evans won as he had known he would.

"Oh . . . thank you, Sergeant. I guess you and I are going to be together for some time, Evans. Can you suggest anything else that I need?"

"You need a new sergeant, sir," said Evans.

"Oh . . . oh, of course. You're going with General Dennis?"

"No, sir, he won't take me." Evans knew he was saying too much but the anger inside him forced the words out. "He says they use colonels for errand boys in Washington. I'm going to China."

Garnett digested this slowly before his face darkened.

"So *you're* going to China? You sound as if this war's a Cook's tour. What do you think this army is anyway, Sergeant?"

"I'd rather not answer that question, sir. But I've done my twenty-five here. I'm entitled to rotation and War Department Circular six nine five three eight dash seven one says applications for the Fortieth Air Army from graduate gunners of this theater will be accepted. The circular and my papers are on your desk, sir."

"Oh. . . ." Garnett realized that he was whipped. He began to perceive that the loss of Evans would save him many such whippings.

"Well of course if the circular authorizes it . . . Can you get me a good man for duty in here?"

"I've been training one, sir; an excellent man. Graduate gunner, very sober and reliable. A Corporal Herbert McGinnis."

"Good. I'll talk to him later."

"There's just a couple of points about it, sir. The T. O. calls for Tech stripes for this job . . ."

"He'll be promoted as he deserves," said Garnett shortly.

"And he should be billeted off the station, sir."

"Isn't that irregular for an enlisted man?"

"Yes, sir. But in this job a man hears and sees a good deal. He shouldn't spend too much time among the other men."

"I see. Where could he be billeted?"

"I've arranged that, sir, in the village. He's interviewing the people now."

"Oh . . . well, I hope he's as capable as you are, Evans."

"So do I, sir. Does the General need anything else?"

"Ask Colonel Haley to step in."

Like Evans, Garnett did not want to be alone. He, too, knew that sooner or later he would have to think of the things that had happened. He would even have to think of how and why they had happened. He jumped from the desk now and circled the room angrily, averting his eyes from the Swastika-shaped fighter cross as he went. It was folly, madness, to try to think such things through. Poor Casey himself was an example of a man who had thought too much.

There were times and places for it but this was not

either. On a staff a man could afford to think; he was expected to. Around him there were always the balance of other men, the weighing of opinion, the checking over every detail before thought went upward for the pen stroke that made it command.

Here he was command. The army had provided him with a staff to think for him in every foreseeable category of human affairs. The obvious problems of life had been precalculated, their conduct codified into regulations that existed to forestall thought and to obviate the human differences in it. Even the unforeseeable dilemmas of the war itself had been divided and parceled out into directives. His own were tidily packaged in the thick folder Casey had turned over to him this afternoon. He was not here to think. He was here to execute those directives. He walked over and touched the folder itself for reassurance.

"You sent for me, sir?" asked Haley from the door.

"Good evening, Haley. Any messages?"

"General Endicott and General Salmond have sent their compliments and will await your decision before planning tomorrow's mission, sir."

It was there, in his face, before he even had time to consider it thoughtfully. He clutched the directive folder and wondered if Haley's imperturbable stare could see the uncertainty inside him.

"Is there anything from General Kane?"

"No, sir."

"I suppose, on a tricky reading, he might wait for twenty hundred weather developments?"

"He might, sir."

The man's impassivity was maddening. "Well, we haven't got *our* twenty hundred weather yet."

"Davis is marking the map, sir. If you'd like to speak to him immediately . . ."

"No, no. Have you final figures from today yet?"

"Posted, sir," said Haley and led the way to the board. In this, too, there was respite. Garnett tried to follow closely but Haley went rapidly, too rapidly, through the details; he found himself missing the significance of it in his dread of the end.

"Thirty-nine lost and four in the Channel and . . . what's this?"

"Category E, sir. Fourteen damaged beyond economical repair."

"So we really lost fifty-seven today?"

"We salvage the crews from those Category E's, sir."

He had a sudden vision of the landing he had seen that afternoon. There had been no crashes today but he was remembering the way the ambulances backed up to the waistgates and the way the uninjured men had climbed out afterward, lowering their feet slowly as if they did not expect them to reach the ground.

"Do we fly those Category E crews tomorrow?"

"All but the wounded, sir. We need them."

Haley turned from the board with finality and waited, his face expectant. Time was passing.

"I don't see how they take it," said Garnett. "What about morale, Haley?"

"There's been no report of trouble, sir."

Garnett remembered without joy that he would be eating three meals a day with this man through an indefinite future. But the prospect of having Haley leave the room now seemed worse. He smiled.

"Haley, we're going to be together a long time, I hope. It would make life simpler if you'd call me Cliff."

"Very well, sir . . . Cliff."

"What do these crews really think about?"

"Their twenty-fifth mission, sir."

"Of course, but what else?"

Haley cogitated. "The normal things, sir, and promotion and decoration, too."

"By the normal things you mean . . . ?" He risked a wider smile and this time it was rewarded by a decorous counterpart from his Chief of Staff.

"Yes, sir. Fortunately the villages are full of it."

"I should think it would lead to trouble."

But the smile was gone now. Haley considered his answer for Accuracy and Completeness.

"Just the normal kinds, sir. These women have been at war a long time. They know the men have to be back for missions."

"Is this . . . immorality very widespread?"

"Very, sir," said Haley. "If it wasn't for the accent you couldn't tell 'em from Americans."

Garnett knew that they were coming to the end of this and he could feel the pressure of the questions that lay beyond; again he fought them off.

"So that kind of morale takes care of itself?"

"Yes, sir. Keeps down perversion, too," said Haley briskly. He waited a respectful interval before letting Garnett feel the compulsion of his slight movement toward the status board again.

"If you're ready to go through tomorrow's status . . . ?"

"Haley, will the change of command in the Division affect morale?"

"It will cheer them up for a while, sir."

"They won't necessarily be hostile to a new face?"

"All generals look alike to them . . . Cliff."

"Then how will it cheer them up?"

"They figure a new general's always good for a couple of soft missions, sir."

Garnett searched that round face for the telltale smirk of an insinuation but it was not there. Haley had been stating a fact. Then, with a surge of relief, he saw Evans with a paper.

"Is that from General Kane?" he snapped.

"No, sir. The last group reports all crews now provided with freshly packed parachutes in compliance with this morning's order, sir."

Disappointment, and the shock of this reminder, seemed to paralyze his tongue. By long habit he nodded curtly and watched Evans disappear. Then, for the first time since he had been in the island, a blessed inner prompting reminded him that the other Generals Garnett must have been in tough places, too.

"We'll go through tomorrow's status, Haley."

There was refuge, even in that arithmetic, and Garnett found himself following with concentration almost to the end before the revelation struck him. He had to clear his throat to be sure eagerness did not lighten his crisp, official tone.

"One thirty and one thirty-two crews. That's not really four full groups, is it?"

"This is the third day of intensive Ops, sir. I bet the Germans would be glad to show 90 per cent service-ability for tomorrow."

"I wasn't criticizing, Haley. But we just haven't the strength General Dennis had, have we?"

"One thirty's enough for any target in the book if they hit it, sir," replied Haley evenly.

"How many crews would be on their last mission?"

"Sixteen, sir."

"Is there any way we could give them a break?"

Haley shook his head slowly; it was an old question but all commanders asked it. "They're your Element, Squadron, Group, and Wing leaders now, sir. Of course if it's a short mission tomorrow that is a break for them, to finish on an easy one."

He waited again but General Garnett said nothing. After a minute he looked at his watch pointedly. But Garnett had gone back to the desk from which he now brought the directive folder.

"Haley, when General Dennis handed over to me this afternoon I missed some of the details. Now, it says here: 'In the absence of explicit target designation or other order from Higher Headquarters, Division Commanders will exercise their own discretion . . .'"

He tossed the folder back onto the desk.

"When should this designation come down?"

"From General Kane's eighteen hundred weather conference, sir."

"In *practice* does he ever wait for later readings?"

"Very rarely, sir."

"If we hear nothing this applies automatically?"

"Automatically, sir."

Haley looked at his watch and permitted himself to shuffle one foot ever so slightly. Patience with new commanders was part of his job but the other parts were piling up in the back room.

"Haley, if General Kane should order us to give these

crews a break, in view of the last three days, the target itself would still be my discretion?"

"Yes, sir. That's in the directive."

"What kind of target would be right for that?"

"That's a matter for Intelligence, sir. If you'd like to speak to Major Lansing . . . ?"

"I want a general idea from you first."

It was improper but a lifetime in the service had shown Haley no way around the ordered improprieties of commanding generals. He led Garnett to the map.

"The Germans probably wouldn't fight for anything in France tomorrow, sir. They'd like a rest, too."

"And there are sound naval objectives in France, aren't there?" Garnett encouraged him. "What about flak?"

"Brest is rough, sir. As for the others I haven't the exact data in my head . . ."

"Just give me a general idea." It was a command.

"Well, sir. Havre is about three point nine, Cherbourg about three point four, Calais about two point two, Dunkirk one point six, Dieppe one point four . . ."

"These are percentages of loss?" breathed Garnett.

"Expectancy, sir, based on previous experience."

"And we have attacked such objectives before?"

Haley shrugged. "For training new crews, sir. If you'd like to speak to Major Lansing . . ."

He turned from the map deliberately now to disclaim further responsibility for the proper spheres of the staff sections. It was not his business.

"I'll see him later," said Garnett. "What about those pictures of today's strikes?"

It was one of the things Haley had wished to accelerate downstairs instead of wasting his time here, but he kept the indignation out of his voice.

"They're rushing them, sir; should be up soon. I doubt if they'll show anything but smoke after that lead group anyway. And you're aware, sir, that both reconnaissance planes are unreported again today."

He was aware; whichever way he turned the whole question was waiting for him.

"Yes, but they're great pictures. It was a wonderful strike, wasn't it?"

"Best of the war, to date, sir."

"None of the later pictures showed parachutes?"

"None, sir."

"And nothing further from crew interrogations?"

"One more sighting that agreed exactly with the others, sir. As the fire worked toward his gas tanks Colonel Martin's plane swung away from the formation and then exploded. Four parachutes were seen to open but there were no individual identifications."

It was impossible to get away from it. Garnett ordered Haley to bring the weather when it was ready and watched the door close with the most acute feeling of loneliness he had ever known. He tried an unhappy circuit of the room but from every angle the Swastika on the wall seemed to draw his eyes. The other Generals Garnett were very far away now. He threw himself into the chair and sat, frowning savagely at the directive folder.

He was staring intently without seeing a letter of the type when Dennis walked in on him. Garnett sprang up with relief only to feel it congealing inside him as he saw that Dennis had on his trench coat and was carrying his cap under his arm. He spoke in quick protest against their purport.

"Come in, Casey. Come in and sit down."

"Isn't my plane reported yet?"

He explained that the special plane which Kane had ordered for Dennis was not due until twenty hundred, noting from his watch as he spoke that there would be at least five minutes until he was finally alone.

"You'd better sit down, Casey. You can't go without those pictures anyway. They're rushing them."

"Yeah. I'd forgotten how to be a courier."

It was the first direct comment on his dismissal Dennis had offered and the bitterness of it burned. All afternoon they had worked together on the mechanics of handing over the command with the impersonal efficiency of their training. But it was done; the soldiers were face to face with the men inside them.

"General Kane's right about your taking the strike photos back, Casey. They'll help Washington understand what you've been through."

Dennis said nothing. The silence, haunted for Garnett now with the questions that lay beyond it, was worse than any subject.

"It's different back there, Casey. Those jobs are tough but it's not like being face to face with it."

"I never was," said Dennis. "Ted did that for me."

"You took the responsibility, though. Those pictures will help you explain."

"All discredited commanders explain. Maybe I'll write a book about it in some quiet back room."

"There can be two points of view about this, Casey."

"So I've learned."

Garnett had a feeling that those eyes were dissecting him, cutting away layer after layer of the pretenses over

247

the turmoil inside him. But before his dry tongue could protest Dennis seemed to relax; his voice was suddenly apologetic under its gruffness.

"I'm sorry, Cliff. I'm taking Ted's personal stuff to Helen."

"Good. You found everything?"

"Everything but his toothbrush."

Garnett shot an uneasy glance at him but Dennis's eyes were on the map. Turning, Garnett found his own vision confronted again with the red crayon cross through Schweinhafen. He averted his eyes.

"You'll go to see Helen at once?"

"Of course." Abruptly Dennis was back in the room with him and his voice had become almost friendly.

"Nothing since the group report, I suppose?"

"One more sighting that agreed exactly with the others. Four parachutes seen. That's something."

"Four chances out of ten."

The statement was flat with the finality that has dismissed hope. They both knew the odds against Martin's position in the plane were smaller than even this tantalizing fragment of chance. Garnett could feel Dennis congealing again. He blurted quickly: —

"Will you say the proper things for me, Casey?"

"What are they?"

"Well, he was doing what he thought was right . . . and so were you."

"And he gets killed and I get canned and Goering gets his jets."

"Casey we're not *sure* he's killed. How do the Germans really treat their prisoners?"

"All right . . . usually."

248

3

Colonel Haley knew that he had seen too many commanders replaced in his time to be disturbed by the process. An order was an order. What was more, Haley had strong feelings about Criticism of Higher Command. Tonight, however, he regretted that this transition had not been accomplished more briskly.

Changes did produce personal tension and while General Dennis would never let his rank down, General Garnett's agitation was so apparent that it would be unsuitable for any of the others to see it.

Entering the office, Haley informed them that the plane for General Dennis had landed and would be gassed in ten minutes. The pictures would be ready by then and General Dennis's effects were being loaded as instructed. Dennis nodded absently but Garnett broke in with that same evident anxiety.

"You're sure there are no messages, Haley?"

"Relay on a cable for General Dennis, sir. Mrs. Dennis and the children will be at the airport at his Estimated Time of Arrival."

"Oh." Haley always forgot how that fleeting smile could take a decade off Dennis's face, for a minute. "Thanks, Ernie."

Haley withdrew but before the door was fully closed Garnett saw Dennis's smile sharpen into that piercing scrutiny he dreaded. He spoke quickly.

"You may not believe this but I envy you, Casey."

"You should." Dennis seemed to relax a little again. "I'm afraid I've been talking like a heel, Cliff. Don't worry about me. I'll duck Washington."

"What will you do?"

Dennis had not allowed himself to think of it consciously yet but it was waiting, formulated in the background of his mind. Full consideration of it now touched him with pity for Garnett. He tried not to let his voice convey his overwhelming relief.

"I guess I still rate a training command. I'll get one where I can have Cathy and the kids with me, where I can get a day off now and then to take the boy fishing. And at night, by God, I'll sleep."

"Casey, will you ask Natalie to send me a bottle of sleeping tablets, large?"

Before he had to answer that Haley and Davis hurried in with the weather map. It was like a relapse into a bad dream after too brief consciousness. Even as he told himself it was no longer his worry he could feel his stomach muscles tensing, could hear Garnett ask the question that was on his own lips.

"Well, what is it?"

Davis spread the map on the table and before he could stop himself Dennis was hanging over it with the rest of them in taut scrutiny of the symbols.

"That front is still slowing down, sir," Davis concluded. "The entire Continent will be open for bombing all day and you'll have until seventeen hundred over the bases."

Dennis did not realize that he was already looking at the other map; he did not even hear the words that came clearly from his own lips.

"My God! I wouldn't have needed parachutes."

Then, he was aware of the silence, of Garnett's start and the stiffening and looks of the others.

250

"Haley," said Garnett, "you're sure there's no word from General Kane?"

"Messages are brought as received, sir."

Dennis controlled himself until they had left the room, whispering savagely under his breath that it was not his business. But with the closing of the door the flooding bitterness inside him opened his mouth involuntarily.

"Well, is it Dieppe or Dunkirk?"

"It's easy for you to talk," retorted Garnett. "You're out of it."

"Left you a horrid example, too, didn't I?"

He knew this was wanton cruelty, but he knew too that like all cruelty it proceeded only from the inner pain that drove it out of him. He should be done with that pain now; he had borne it long enough along with the rest of the burden. But he could not be done with it until Garnett assumed it.

"I didn't mean it that way, Casey. I'm trying to think of the crews."

"What crews?"

"My . . . the combat crews. They've just been through the worst three days of the war. Sixteen of them would finish tomorrow and go home, to their families, free."

"You'd better think of the others."

"What others?"

"The ones who'll have to replace those sixteen and all others who'll have to come after them if these don't do their job."

"Casey, that's in the future, it's abstract. . . ."

"It's what you're paid to think about. After you've done it try thinking about the infantry, going up those

251

beaches on D-Day against jet fighter bombers that have already whipped us."

He could see Garnett recoiling and part of him could pity the man, but it was the part he had whipped too often and too mercilessly in himself. There was no place for pity in this; there would be no escape for himself until he had driven Garnett beyond it.

"I did think of it that way in Washington," said Garnett. "But after yesterday and today, watching those ambulances, and the stretchers coming out of the planes, hearing the boys ask about tomorrow's weather before they hit the ground . . ."

He paused, but there was no comfort in the bleak face before him and he went on with rising vehemence.

"I've had to think of Ted over there, dead or maybe wounded and hiding . . . or captured . . . and my own sister not knowing . . ."

"He's damned lucky," said Dennis, "and so are you. You wanted a B-29 command. You wanted to take him where the Japs torture captured crews for fun. Out there you wouldn't have any Kane to save your sanity for you with orders to take it easy."

"Casey, he hasn't sent me any orders."

Dennis had known this. It had been waiting for him as he entered the room, leering from Garnett's manifest agitation, taunting him through their guarded silences, shrieking at him from the questions Garnett had asked Haley. Even more than Garnett himself Dennis had been dreading it. He had denied it to himself. He wanted only to escape, to get into that plane and go.

He had earned his freedom; he should be free. He had

252

forced this test to the breaking point and been broken. He had failed and been fired. It was over. He should have nothing to face but the future now; there was more than enough in that.

He had to learn to live with the vacuum that had been Ted. He had to get himself together to dissemble agreement, to feign comfort from Cathy's consolations and reassurances. He had to find work, to rededicate himself, to get a training command where his skills and experience could re-enter the inexorable continuity of the army's purposes and contribute still.

All of this was before him. He had set his face and steps and thought toward it, but now he saw that it was another step away, that he could not yet put down the burden of the present. He was gathering himself under it slowly when Haley plodded in apologetically with the package of pictures.

"And there's a phone call for General Garnett . . ."

"From General Kane?"

"No, sir. A minor disciplinary matter. I'll be glad to attend to it with the General's authority. One of our men has broken a window in the village and the owner insists upon speaking to the commanding general. I can handle it for you, sir."

Dennis waited, reabsorbing strength from the weight of the burden itself as Garnett retreated eagerly into this.

"Broke a window, did he. Drunk, too, I suppose?"

"No complaint of that, sir," said Haley scrupulously. "Statement was he broke the window jumping through it. Damage upward of thirty shillings. I'll be glad to attend to it, sir, with authorization."

"Send him to me," said Garnett. "I'll teach him to jump into windows."

"Complaint was he broke it jumping *out*, sir."

"EVANS!" shouted Dennis.

The Sergeant appeared in the door, clicking his heels to wary attention.

"What did you do at the Magruder's?" barked Dennis.

"Just what was expected, sir. I give them the ice cream, too."

"Did you break a window there today?"

"I . . . I ain't been there today, sir." But they all saw him suppress a quick start of comprehension.

"Did you send someone else?"

"Sir," said Evans, "I had a verbal directive from the General authorizing me to delegate . . ."

Pounding feet stampeded through the anteroom, the door burst open, and Corporal McGinnis crashed in on them. He was bleeding slightly from cuts on his hands and face but his righteous wrath was oblivious of the wounds as it was of the officers in the room. His eyes were fixed upon Evans.

"Protection! They needed *protection!* And me a married man! I bet I protect you!"

He was advancing on Evans with mayhem in his eyes when Garnett recovered enough to catch him.

"Who in hell are you?"

"Corporal Herbert McGinnis, sir." The enormity of his intrusion was dawning upon McGinnis.

"Evans, is this the sober, reliable man you're getting me?"

"Sir," said McGinnis indignantly, "I joined the army to *fight* for my country . . ."

"SHUT UP, YOU!" thundered Haley. "General, if you'll let me attend to this."

"I think you'd better," said Garnett.

He turned from the closing door for the relief of laughter, but there was no laughter in Dennis's face.

"Kane *hasn't* ordered a milk run?"

"No. He hasn't ordered anything. Of course I know what he expects of me . . ."

"What do you expect of yourself?"

He saw Garnett squirm and then, as the remark bit more deeply into him, it found a tougher substructure. His reply was angry, combative.

"It's easy for you to talk. When you had to decide this last night Kane was here, supporting you."

"Was he in that lead plane this morning, supporting Ted?"

Haley, returning just then with the message from General Kane, thought Garnett looked better. His face was red with anger but there was a new tone in his curt command for Haley to read the signal aloud.

" 'General Kane and party,' " he read, " 'compelled proceed Hemisphere Commander's dinner for guests London consequently unable attend weather conference. General Kane desires express especial confidence in General Garnett's discretion based on weather. Other divisions notified. Signed Saybold for Kane.' "

Haley raised his head expectantly. Through the silence they could all hear the muffled droning of motors outside and the clattering of the teleprinter. But still neither Garnett nor Dennis spoke.

"The group commanders need briefing poop and bomb loads for tomorrow, sir," said Haley.

255

Garnett appeared not to have heard him. His face and forehead were heavily furrowed now. He stirred and quoted, half aloud: —

" 'Especial confidence General Garnett's discretion . . .' Casey, this isn't permission . . ."

"It's just what Ted had this morning," said Dennis. "He could be here right now, sitting in that chair, on his discretion."

"That was different," said Garnett slowly. "By the time he got it he was already committed. He probably didn't have any real choice."

"What do you think he took that toothbrush for?" demanded Dennis. "When he left here this morning he knew Kane would pass the buck to him."

For a second more Garnett hesitated, whispering to himself that he must think. But in the echoing silence of his mind he knew it was evasion. Thought itself would only be evasion. He shook his head hard to clear it.

"Haley, notify the other divisions and all groups that the Fifth Division will attack Fendelhorst."

Dennis scarcely saw Haley's departure. There had come over him a sense of soaring, giddy lightness; he seemed to be floating in detachment. He knew it for what it was, the lifted disequilibrium of final release from a crushing load. When his senses readjusted themselves to it this time he would be free. He would walk to the plane lightly and get into it and go. None of this could follow him now.

He found that he was shaking hands with Garnett, who was grinning at him a little wryly.

"Save me a job in that training command, will you?"

256

"You'll be wanting it," said Dennis, and he knew that Garnett could understand him.

"And don't forget those sleeping tablets."

He nodded casually before remembering that he and Garnett were past that now.

"Cliff, they're no good. I didn't think you'd need to know this but — you know Major Dayhuff . . . I introduced him to you this afternoon."

"Dayhuff . . . Dayhuff . . . ? Oh, sure. My ordnance man. Nice fellow."

"No. Your medical officer. Pretty nice fellow. He'll help you, but not enough."

He saw Garnett nod slow acceptance and began to fasten the little catches on his coat collar. His hands were not altogether sure and his feet felt light, but every minute was with him now. The entrance of Evans quickened his reawakening with a flicker of the familiar pain he had known in other partings.

"The plane's ready, sir, and . . . good luck."

He shook hands more rapidly than he meant to but he could see, in Evans's face, that it was all right. Garnett had put on a cap to go out with him and Evans was standing back to let them pass when Haley came in.

"Sir," he said reluctantly, "there's an order for General Dennis from Washington."

A look at Haley's troubled face told him. He could feel the whole burden again now, crushing down on him through the Colonel's silent hesitancy; he could see a reflection of it in the shocked comprehension in Garnett's eyes.

"No! I've got my orders, Haley. I've gone home."

"We're instructed to relay this to your plane, sir."

257

He wanted to refuse it, to run for the plane, but his feet would not move. He watched Haley walk over, a little uncertainly, and hand the paper to Garnett. It gave him a few seconds to brace himself, to set his feet, though he still could not feel them. Garnett wet his lips and read slowly: —

" 'With immediate effect General Dennis will proceed via Gibraltar, Cairo, Karachi, and Calcutta to Chungking to await imminent arrival his B-29 Command.' "

Against the first full shock of it he heard himself shout. "No, by God . . . !"

Then instinctive, immediate shame choked his outburst and followed it into the silence. He found that his hands were steady on the catches of his coat collar now. He could feel his legs, all the way to the floor, and they were not buckling. The quick, upsurging roar of a warming motor outside seemed to transmit some of its own power into him. As the sound faded he could feel his new burden fully, but this time his strength was under it; the equilibrium was restored.

"Cliff, does that say 'with immediate effect'?"

"I'm afraid it does, Casey."

"Evans," he said sharply, "get your things."